Praise

For the first time in print Nicole opens herself up to share her story with so much vulnerability, while leaving her readers feeling inspired, captivated and leaves their minds reeling towards their own truth and healing.

Such an amazing and well written book that you won't want to put down until the end.

Cathy Davis

I could not put this book down!! As I was reading The Greater Plan I felt like Nicole was talking directly to me. I felt all the feels throughout this book, I laughed and cried, I was spooked, excited and horrified. After I finished, it really hit home that you have no idea of what people go through in their lives and we really need to be kinder and understanding of each other. Even if we don't know their backgrounds. An amazing read, I highly recommend it to all!

Dawne Recker

Very moving story. The love Nicole has for her son and resilience shines through. Words written by Nicole will stay with and motivate readers incredibly. It was an honor to read her life story and learn the lessons she finds most valuable.

D. Sarah

Nicole Recker takes the reader on a journey that teaches how the hardest times of your life can end up creating the most meaning for our successes. In this intimate telling Nicole bares her soul, sharing with the reader her most difficult times and how each one was ultimately a stepping stone on a greater path and a lesson to be learned. This story about hardship, trauma and loss will stir emotion and ultimately leave the reader with lessons about some of the most important things in life: love, family, growth and healing. In her own voice, as a mother, Nicole's story carries meaning for mothers, fathers, sons and daughters alike, in a way that anyone can relate to.

Chris Recker

Nicole captures hardship, inspiration, realism and strength all in one story. It's an absolute must read that you're not going to want to put down!

Tiffany Davis

"The Greater Plan" by Nicole Recker is a raw and vulnerable look into Nicole's journey in life, the ability to overcome, push forward and show optimism through trauma, struggle and when our lives and plans don't end up the way we envisioned – but for a "greater plan". Nicole bares pieces of her soul and insightful reflections and strategies to build one's self esteem, bravery and tenacity to keep pushing for and towards our dreams. A heartfelt sharing of Nicole's life journey to and in Motherhood, struggles with fertility, loss (trigger warning) and the ability to push on with grace, thankfulness and courage. Thank you for your amazing soul, Nicole.

Joy Lonsdale – Calkins, C.Y.C.W. & Mother

The Greater Plan will change you. Nicole takes you on her journey of healing and asks you to bravely join her. It's a story of strength and resilience as she shares defining moments of connection, innocence, trauma, courage, loss, gratitude and love. You won't want to stop reading, because her story will give you a new appreciation of life.

Nicki Foti Di Gravina

THE GREATER PLAN

Enjoy the read and I hope you feel connection along the way!

Along with enjoying the journey I take you on to discover 'The Greater Plan' for you!

With Gratitude,

Nicole Becker!

THE GREATER PLAN

WITHIN THE LESSONS
THE REASONS WERE FOUND

NICOLE RECKER

The Greater Plan

Within the Lessons the Reasons Were Found

ISBN: 978-1-7782125-0-5 Paperback

To my Son: For all the days that come your way,
know I will always guide you.

CONTENTS

Be like a Buffalo.

In the wild, when a storm comes, all the other animals run away from the storm. By doing this, the storm chases them. Making them stay with the storm longer. The Buffalo are the only animals that choose to run directly into the storm. Making the Buffalo pass through the storm faster.

Being like a Buffalo, I realized, is to focus on things I can control rather than what I can't. Sometimes running head-on into the most difficult times in life is what needs to be done.

1

NOTHING GROWS WHERE NOTHING IS PLANTED

One summer, I planted twelve sunflower seeds in total. Six in pots that I started early inside and eventually moved outside. The other six seeds I planted right in the ground outside in the spring.

All the seeds were cared for in the exact same way. The same amount of light and water, the only difference was the space in which they grew. The space responsible for their roots.

What I found at the end of the summer was actually mind-blowing.

The sunflowers in my flower pots grew two feet tall and some produced a small flower head but not one of these sunflowers actually opened.

While the sunflowers in my front garden grew from a range of four to ten feet tall, *every single* plant produced a flower and opened beautifully.

My biggest lessons and takeaways from this experience are:

- The area we sometimes choose to grow in or are planted into can be *exactly* what hinders us from growing into our truest potential and what sucks the life out of us.
- Not allowing ourselves the space to be our best selves can hinder this potential.
- The roots when taken out from the pots were tight, compacted and smothering themselves. The pots were preventing the sunflowers from having space to expand and grow.
- The roots from the plant were expanding and reached deep into the earth allowing for the sunflower to stand strong. Creating a strong foundation that made the sunflower plant withstand anything that tried to destroy it.

Be mindful and aware of the place you're *choosing* to grow in and take a moment to ask yourself, is this the place where I can thrive? Think hard about this because you deserve to be in a place where you can thrive so much that your future self will thank you for all the hard work you put in.

Can you recall a situation or time in your life that something happened and years later you figured out the meaning, almost as if life has a greater purpose for our experiences? Maybe it was a time where you couldn't believe the situation was happening to, or for you. Yet now, it has such an important role in shaping who you are?

Well, I have and I am here to tell you that if you have experienced this, you are *not* alone. Through our time together I will share my life experiences that at these moments in time,

I may not have understood why they were happening for me but by the end of this book you'll figure out how it all was part of the greater plan.

Now before we get started, I want to be clear that I am forever grateful for everything that has led me to where I am today, the happy, the magical, the sad, the traumatic and all the feels in between. I am who I am today because of them all.

I am stronger because of each moment but most importantly the moments where I decided to keep going and be proud of who I was. And my younger self would be so proud, because the woman I rose to be is not the one I imagined, she is everything and more.

I truly believe sometimes we are running away from our truest selves that we were born to be. Trust in ourselves and surrender while trusting in the process.

Let me ask you another question. If you could go back to your younger self. What would you say?

Take a moment to do this.

Now knowing what you know now. What would you say to your present self?

Would you have words of encouragement, complete joy, gratitude, love and kindness for everything you've been through and the person you've become? I hope so. You are alive, you are an absolute miracle on this earth and I am so excited to spend time together through this journey called life. I hope something I share can remind you of the inner strength we all have within but may never know existed, that true love does exist, life can give you such magical moments you wish you could bottle them up forever and also moments you wish you never had to relive. True ups and downs. I'm here for it all to be so vulnerable because what I've learned through doing this, is that we as humans can connect through multiple experiences.

2

THE GHETTO LIFE

The things I experienced when growing up as a child felt like something out of a movie some days.

Black ice

One night my family and I were driving home from up north visiting family. It was dark and my mom and I were listening to *Maria Maria* sung by Santana. *Those lyrics still get me every time.* My mom hit black ice with my uncle and aunt following behind us along with my sister and me in the car with her. She spun us around so that she would be the one to hit the guardrail and not us. I remember when the car stopped my mom put her hand on my chest and asked, "Are you okay?" I said I was scared and she reassured me that we were all okay but not to get upset and wake my sister. I can still see the black marks all over the guardrail. This man stopped to ask if we were all okay while my mom checked outside the vehicle. Meanwhile, my uncle parked behind us to protect us from traffic. We were okay, the car was beaten up but that was the least of my mom's worries. We continued driving home and were pulled over by a police car. The policeman told my mom he had heard we were in an accident and the man who stopped to see if we were okay called the police and said my mom was loaded drunk, which he later found out was a lie and his time was wasted. I had to sit in our car as he took my mom to his back seat, terrified, all while my sister slept through the entire thing. This moment shocked me. I couldn't comprehend how one second everything was normal and in a matter of seconds everything changed.

Gun shots

My mom used to have a home daycare while I was growing up and we would do daily activities and events. She would take care of children of all ages, and one day we were taking public transit home from the Toronto zoo. The bus was loud, but I'm pretty sure the noise was all from us. My mom, at the time, was doing anything possible to keep a handful of kids quiet and god help her. She was an incredible superhero then and still is.

We arrived at our stop, my mom gathered us all together and made our way off the bus, then we heard gunshots. A man had shot another person on the bus and there it was, all for us to see.

My mom continued trying to keep us all moving so we would pay no attention to what the heck just happened.

Police practice

One day my mom, sister, daycare kids and I were walking to school to find what looked like blood on the wall of the school and an outline of a body. We were later told by the school that the police were practicing with paintball guns on how to react to a stressful situation. Looking back on this, kids will believe anything.

The old Cadillac

One of my mom's daycare kids was a toddler and she loved to place anything inside her nose. She'd place the corner of her blanket up her nose or anything else that would fit. One day my mom had an emergency to handle as the little girl had again placed something she shouldn't have up her nose. I remember this day because it was the first day I had to walk to school alone. While walking to school, I was approached by a Cadillac filled with grown men. One-man opened the door and said, "Hey pretty girl, you should come in our car". I was always taught to never speak to strangers, so my flight radar was pretty strong. I ran as fast as my little legs could run. I made it onto school property, where this man immediately turned away and said "You're lucky today." I don't remember if I told my parents this. I had always heard other kids talking about things that had happened to them. Making this just one of those things that didn't seem like a big deal.

The police chase

The bell rang for recess and all the kids were in the schoolyard. I remember playing under a willow tree with some of my friends. Then two men jumped over the school fence and shortly after two police cars drove straight through the fence and chased these men around the school field. The teachers called us all into the school quickly and recess was called to a quick and very short end. We went back inside and were told that everything was fine, to remain calm and enjoy indoor activities before class started and it was never spoken of again.

The teacher I trusted

When I was in school, I had a teacher who told me my writing wasn't very good, she told me I needed to come to school early in the morning and stay later in the day to improve this skill. Promising that once it improved I could stop coming to see her daily. I trusted this teacher, I looked forward to seeing her every day and she was such a bright light in my world. One day she didn't show up and I was told to not come to school early or stay late as she was no longer a teacher at my school. I had so many new teachers to finish off that year I lost track of how many names I needed to learn. I was so upset that I didn't get to work on something she told me I was going to get better at, but I later found out the truth of this situation.

Hold the key

My grade six teacher was the best teacher I had ever had from this point. We laughed and had so much trust built within our class. I remember some days were filled just with us connecting with each other. I feel that he knew how much some kids had on their plate and wanted to make school a safe and fun place to come. I learnt an interesting lesson at age eleven from him. He told me that if I were to ever get jumped alone to hold a key in between my first and middle finger and not to hold back.

All valuable lessons

Life had a way of teaching me to be cautious at such a young age but all lessons were very valuable for real life, I can most definitely admit that. Going through these events caused me to have difficulty trusting others. Learning to trust myself along with my intuition without letting my self-doubt take over took practice. Controlling my overthinking about every situation along with my spiraling about if each choice I took or someone else was choosing was either positive or negative. Knowing when to let my guard down and showing others my truest self without being concerned about what they would think of me. Grieving, learning to always love your most important people while never taking them for granted. These, along with others, would be things that I would work through at an older age.

3

KIRKER FAMILY

Have you ever been in a place where no one is blood-related but everyone feels like family? That type of bond where everyone has each other's backs? If you needed something no matter what time of day everyone is there for each other?

Well, if you haven't I hope that one day you will! If you have experienced this, isn't it wonderful?

We met on Kirker Ave, a street in the middle of Scarborough, hence why they are called the Kirker family. The street was our backyard where we would create so many memories and build a massive family. We all met when we were young kids. I was the oldest on the street and I was always called mother hen because I would be the young one carrying a baby on my hip.

Growing up in Scarborough, you didn't speak to anyone walking down the street until you got to Kirker Ave.

We had the BEST times here, from blocked off street parties, where everyone just participated and the ones who didn't wouldn't dare say anything about it because they were outnumbered by laughter and jokes.

Everyone loved to gather around a bonfire on the weekends and let's just say our neighbour behind wasn't such a big fan. They would call the fire department so often that when the fire crew showed up they would come by for hot dogs and a good laugh. Maybe the neighbour who called all the time was sadder than anything for never getting invited, but maybe they should have moved to Kirker Ave instead. I'm just kidding, everyone was always welcome. This one neighbour was always so hateful.

Epic Pranks

My goodness, I can still remember the jokes and pranks we would play on each other. Those were some good ol' classic pranks, way before we had google or any other internet sites to research epic pranks. Honestly, I feel some of those pranks you could NEVER get away with now.

Taking your neighbour's entire patio furniture and putting it on the roof of their carport or, how about this one, changing all the numbers on the houses while people weren't home. The poor, unfortunate mailman, probably said a few hurtful words after that prank.

Having one of the other neighbours write up a fake document that stated my dad was going to be fined for a pool he put in without a permit, heart-throbbing, real epic pranks. But the most epic was having my dad and a couple of others take apart another neighbour's shed and put it into someone else's back yard for weeks, making the other neighbour believe someone stole it. Aren't those some crazy pranks? Would you pull those pranks on someone you know? I know for sure I wouldn't be able to where I'm currently living.

Food fight

Then, there were the food fights! We were always laughing and clowning around with Kirker individuals and we all had a sense of humor. We had a party at my neighbour's place and then it started, that first handful of food was thrown, what the actual F. It was like a movie. I couldn't believe it. People were running all around taking handfuls of whatever they could grab. Never mind chasing people all around who thought they could escape. I remember running down the entire street so fast with no shoes on just to try to get away, later, to be met with the water hose for the lack of food on me, along with some of the smaller kids. Yes, all ages were part of this food fight.

Pool party

The pool parties were endless. We were either having bonfires, having street parties or were in the pool. And if you weren't willing to be part of those, well, you just ended up being included. The pool parties were the easiest to forcefully make others be a part of as the deck around our pool was the same height as the pool. So no matter what was in your hands, pockets or if you were even dressed for the pool, that didn't matter. There was no saving you!

The kids

Staying with all of these families 90% of the time, their kids became all of our newest members. The parents seemed most excited because it was another way to give them some time alone. God, love them for the amount of dance shows our parents had to watch. All but one of us were girls. These kids all became part of our family, they were thrown right into an intense connection of love, laughter and bond that would stay with us for life. Almost all of us talk to this very day. Staying connected with each other's big moments.

Once in a lifetime

I'll never forget the day that the first person put up a for sale sign. Just like anything it was a ripple effect. When we parted with this street, it was so strange because, for most of my life, I was raised on this street and I thought everyone got to experience this sense of community. Until we moved and I realized the connection, family, trust and bond was so rare. I have spent my time, still to this moment, thinking and wishing for one more food fight, one more bonfire, one more pool party with all of these lovely people. It was a bond like no other.

So, if you still have connections with people where no one is blood-related but everyone feels like family. The bond where everyone has each other's backs. When you need something no matter what time of day and everyone else is there. Be grateful, call them, walk outside, say hey and, most importantly, build the memories because you're luckier than most.

Maybe use this as inspiration to be kinder to the neighbour(s) you have, let the walls down a little, laugh and build memories with the ones around you. Because hey? We're all living this life and it's better lived when we are connected with others, just like family!

4

TRAGEDY THAT LED ME HOME

The bullying that I experienced throughout my younger years ranged from harmful jokes to moments that would shake my entire world, some of which still haunt me. This was by far the hardest chapter and time in my life to look back on. You may wonder why because I haven't always found or chosen courage. The courage to tell many people in my life about this, and courage to not care about others' thoughts or opinions. Even for you reading this, this very well may be the first-*ever* time you're reading this part of my story. Before I get into this though, even though I haven't shared with many, I am forever grateful for all of my experiences, including this one, despite how hard they are to look back on. I also know that my parents did the best they could for me.

So you may be thinking, then why even bother putting it in your book Nicole? If it's too hard to talk about and no one really knows of it, why share?

Don't worry, I only know this thought because I have also thought this.

But what I have learned through my healing journey is that I can heal my past by sitting with a magnifying glass and viewing them from another perspective. Learn the lessons being taught because then they will stop coming around. Also, big picture thought here, it's not only about me. Sharing our most dearest stories can leave room to allow and help others heal.

So I am cringing, thinking about writing this here for whoever wants to read it. But I'm staring fear straight in the face and screaming, not today. So here goes!

I will bring you back to a time where I was eleven years old. The wounds are still very deep for me as I'm in my thirties and still feel so nervous to spill the beans.

I was being bullied a lot and not just verbally but physically too. So much that I couldn't handle going to school. I would tell my mom that I was too sick to go so I could avoid that place. I was petrified to tell my parents the truth in fear of what would happen to me.

I was only able to do this for so long until my mom caught on. To be honest, when I look back on this moment I can't remember everything as there are a lot of broken pieces.

I remember one day, very specifically though, it was the end of the day and time to go home. My mom had the daycare at the time so when it was the end of the day I always loved being able to go home and help my mom take care of the kids.

I started towards the stairwell. My school was on the bigger side, with floors on the upper and lower level. To leave there was a staircase that had a landing, after a couple of stairs there was another flight of stairs to go down, after the second flight of stairs there was an exit on the right to get out of the school.

I started at the top, I could hear a voice coming towards me. It was him.

He was laughing and joking around. He pushed me down the stairs only for me to catch my balance and for him to come running after me. He pushed me down the second flight of stairs, picked me up and hit my head against the brick wall.

I gave it my all to try and run away. But there was no one in the staircase but the two of us. Keep in mind this child was also eleven years old.

He grabbed my arm or backpack I can't really remember like I said parts of my memory for this aren't always clear.

He held a gun to the right side of my head and a knife to my throat and said in my left ear, "Your mom is going to watch me kill you today."

I looked through the glass window in the door that exited outside. I never wanted to be in the safety of my mom's arms more than at this moment. I vaguely remember seeing the daycare kids and her coming towards the door.

I was terrified for my life. I immediately thought I was never going to get to experience growing up. Building memories with my family as I saw it was coming to an end. I couldn't do anything about it. I thought about my sister, being able to drive, get married or having a family of my own. I wanted to experience life not just in the mind of an eleven-year-old.

Then, he let go and walked away. I was in such disbelief. I was so terrified and as I remember this moment as I'm writing it here, my legs feel like cement and I want to run but I can't. My heart is racing. The tears are there and sometimes I'm overwhelmed with emotions while other times I can't cry anymore because it feels as though I've dried up the tears that I have left for this. Healing truly does have its confusing moments.

What happened next, you may be thinking. It is so vague in my mind. I wish I could remember it all in detail.

I remember running to my mom, telling her and the next thing we were headed for the principal's office. My mom never swore when we were kids but I heard her say some words that day. I sat in the principal's chair and my mom told her what happened. The principal's response to this day boils my blood. She said, "In the family life this child comes from, unfortunately, this is the way his family shows him love, he is a troubled child and I'm not sure what would happen to him if his family knew about this. So, you get to decide what you want to be done about this." She paused and looked at me.

Sorry, what? You're asking and looking for a response out of me, an eleven-year-old little girl who had her entire world and life flash before her eyes, what do I want to do about this? I remember not saying a word and looking at my mom. My principal then said, "You can choose to press charges and have to go to court and face him." I looked at my mom and said I didn't want to do that because I didn't want to look at him one more time, never mind go to court. My mom replied to the principal, "I want this child kicked out of this school and to never set foot on the premises as long as my daughter goes here."

So we left and that is what happened. Other than finishing my grade six year I don't remember anything else.

My mom and dad made a decision. I needed to change schools after grade six and the school I was to go to next required me to take public transit. I would only be twelve years old and would have to pass a very bad neighbourhood in Scarborough. They wanted my safety to be the main priority. So my childhood home went up for sale and we moved that year. I wouldn't get to see my friends again or the place I once knew but, most importantly, we never spoke of this moment again.

I have no judgement of my parents' decisions, it wasn't right or wrong it just was. But from where I stand now, it was the *best* decision they could have made for me.

I've grieved this chapter of my life every day going forward since the incident happened. As it was one of the most traumatic events that have ever occurred. It made me realize, at the time, my younger self would have traded lives with anyone willing to. As this was too much to handle at times and led me to years of mental confusion, wounds that are most days too deep to handle, unanswered questions and doing my best to forget this event even happened. My younger self had lots of regrets and anger about this time. Regrets of not speaking about being bullied to people sooner because maybe if I did, it wouldn't have gone this far. Regrets of my decision to hide and not be my most genuine self. Anger that this child did this to me. So much anger was found by playing this time over and over of how I could have approached it differently. There is still one real, hit you right in all the feels type of regret, the regret that I never found the courage and strength to face him and press charges. This weighed heavily on my heart due to my lack of strength and courage, maybe, I wasn't the last person he bullied. This caused a lot of internal battles at times because this situation controlled how I lived for so many years. Not realizing that this was far from the right answer for me to be able to start on my journey of healing. Not knowing when the time would ever be right, I know now this tragedy has led me home, while also teaching me to always be grateful for the life I live and every moment going forward.

But what wasn't realized by my younger self in the early stages of healing was the greater plan life had in store.

5

COUNTRY VIBES

The day had come, it was moving day. I remember sitting in the backseat of our car as we drove an hour north of Scarborough with all of our belongings in a transport truck. My parents said we were moving to Beeton, and all I could think was wow, where the heck was my family headed.

I remember being so mad. I didn't want to live in the country but I also knew I didn't want to live in the city either.

As an eleven-year-old with no control over the family choices, I was dragged along. I just couldn't stop wondering where we were moving next.

When I grew up in Scarborough the rules were you didn't speak to strangers and when you were walking past someone you didn't look or stare at them. I was to keep my eyes where I was wanting to go and stay close by.

Now, when we moved to Beeton the moment you walked outside people would be saying hello, how are you? Are you having a good day? I remember walking the main road in town with my dad and people were trying to talk to us and looking straight at us smiling. I said to my dad, "Dad what is wrong with these people, why are they acting strange?" He laughed and said, "They were just being friendly, it's okay." But I was so confused about what was happening.

New surroundings

As we got settled in, it was time to start at our new school. I remember my sister crying about starting a new school, so I knew I needed to be strong for the both of us.

When I sat in my first classroom I was hit so hard in the face with culture shock. Where I grew up, besides my sister and me, there were a handful of others of the same ethnic background. I had friends of all different races and backgrounds in Scarborough. Here everyone was the same, I hated it and I felt like I didn't belong.

I remember telling my parents I hated it here and I wanted to move back. All I ever heard were crickets at night. The evenings were so quiet that our family would have to sleep with a window open just to hear that sound. It was quiet and annoying all at the same time.

But it was a new start and I clearly wasn't going back.

One day during school everyone heard a terrifying alarm. We were randomly brought to the retirement home behind our school and were told we were just practicing a drill. However, we sat at this old age home for hours. When we were finally able to walk back to the school, we realized police had swarmed the area. Growing up I was way too familiar with the sounds of police. We met with my mom and were told that this was a police drill to teach the dogs how to act in difficult environments. Later to find out that this was a bomb threat from other kids at the school.

I remember feeling so mad at my parents, how could they move us away from certain scary experiences to now move us to a school that has bomb threats.

However, I found out later that this was the most excitement this town had in years.

For now, I was just grateful to be home with my family and it be a false alarm for a bomb threat, it was some bored child trying to make a joke.

This town had a very different sense of humor than I was used to but I was willing to give it a try.

Beeton was a little town I hated at first but have grown to love. This was where I was meant to be. This would be my playground for so many future lessons in the years to come.

Moving into a new home had moments of excitement because I was eager to find out more about this place. Not only was I unpacking the house, but I actually stumbled across unpacking some of the past.

One day I found a newspaper article from the previous year. I started to read it and this was how I learnt the truth about why my fifth-grade teacher no longer came back to my school. My mom hid the article to protect me from finding out the truth about what happened to my teacher. The article read that my teacher was in a gang, she robbed banks, she stole and harmed a lot of people. Finding this out is what changed the way I trusted people dramatically. How could someone that I trusted and spent so much alone time with have done wrong to so many people? I remember this pit feeling in my stomach, and thought this was a lie and the things that were printed in that newspaper weren't true. She was so kind to me and she never once made me believe that she would do any harm. The thing I realized is that I was viewing her through my nine or ten-year-old eyes at the time, and what child sees the bad in people?

Little did I know this was going to be a situation that made me always second guess my trust in others and awaken a level of caution that would stay with me in all my future events.

As I mentioned, I hated this little country town before I even gave it a chance, but this is where I would spend my time growing up. I would learn about myself, make new friendships that changed my life, have my first date, first kiss, learn to drive. I would be taught how to drive my first standard vehicle. When I was legal, I'd stumble home drunk from the local pub. I would learn some lessons that were good, bad, sad and terrifying but I'd cherish those moments for all the years to come.

If I knew from the start how many incredible things I would have been given, I would have felt like I had arrived at the place that would grow me into the human being I am today. I have my incredibly brave, courageous, strong, kind and loving parents to thank for all of that. I know that my sister and I were and are always in their best interest and my parents did the absolute best to provide for us.

Sometimes when a place feels like the worst place for you, just pivot and change your thoughts for a moment. Search, even if you have to spend a long time doing so and find the good in everything because maybe, just maybe, life has an even greater plan for you.

6

I'M NOT AS INVINCIBLE AS I THOUGHT

Have you ever experienced your life flash before your eyes?

The mistake that almost cost my life

I wish with every ounce of my body that I could answer this question differently. I was a teenager that loved the feeling of going fast on anything that I was able to. Snowmobiles, quads and unfortunately vehicles. Vehicles, especially when I had an incredible song blaring. The blood would rush through my body when I would go fast with a sense of freedom that I didn't think could hurt me. Well, that was what I thought until one day I realized I was no longer invincible and learned so fast that I had made a terrible decision and my one hope was to survive.

July 7th, 2009 was the day my life flashed before my eyes and would be a day I would NEVER forget.

I got a call that one of my friends had picked up her new car. We worked at a campground and I was working the late shift and would finish around 11:00pm. I told her I would meet her to check out her car once I had finished work.

We lived in the country where the roads were wide open and when you rolled the windows down with nothing but the wind in your hair and a good song, it was easy to speed over the limit. I was blaring the new Lil' Wayne CD, my vehicle at the time had a $2000.00 stereo system that felt like you were inside a club when you put on any song, never mind Lil' Wayne. It was a good time. I was so excited for my friend who had picked up this vehicle and like anyone who loved to drive fast, I was most definitely not being left behind.

I pulled out to pass her once it was clear to do so and at this time of night you were lucky if you saw another car on the road. So we pulled up alongside each other and stomped on it. Nothing could stop me at this age. I only wish there was something that could have.

My friend called me on my cell phone and she told me, "Nicole, it's okay that we were racing on a paved road but let's not race on a gravel one." My words to this day that I said back to her haunt me. I said, "Hahaha yeah right, chicken, I'll race you to the next stop sign."

Gosh, what I would do to go back in time and change what was about to happen next and what I would have said knowing what I know now.

I would have said so many different things. Maybe, "Hey girl, your right thanks for calling me to make sure I didn't do anything stupid."

Or, "Hey girl, what were we thinking in the first place? Racing, in general, is stupid. Of course I wouldn't race on a dirt road."

Maybe, "Hey girl, thanks for valuing my life a little more than I just did a couple minutes ago. We're pretty stupid racing from the beginning. Thanks for having my back, you're a great friend."

Instead, my response was full-out laughter and pure stupidity, "Hahaha yeah right, chicken, I'll race you to the next stop sign." I hung up the phone and stomped my gas pedal to the floor. (Writing this I get a sick feeling in my stomach, only if I got that feeling then.)

How am I alive?

I remember looking down at my speedometer and I was going 120 km on a gravel road. It was about 11:30 pm then. My sick stomach feeling how I wished it had before, had started to kick in. I realized I was going way too fast for a gravel road and I hit my breaks. I actually hit my breaks a couple times because I couldn't get good traction and would swerve every time I did. While I am writing this, I can feel the tears rolling down my cheeks. The next thing I saw was a telephone pole, my car was no longer driving straight down the road, it was facing left. I had *never* been in that position before, my first response was to turn the wheel to the right to try to correct myself but I pulled my steering wheel too much out of sheer panic. This was the worst decision I could have made and the timing of it all couldn't have been worse because I had overcorrected right into a pothole. This sent my vehicle rolling in the air until it stopped.

My first reaction was to turn around and if you've ever driven in the country at 11:35 pm at night there are no street lights in sight and it is pitch black. I remember turning my head around and I couldn't see anything. I immediately thought my friend had just left me there. I then looked back at my steering wheel, I had a ball on my keychain and if it was hit, it would flash. Flipping my car made it go off like crazy. I noticed it was hanging upside down, it was at that moment I realized my car was flipped upside down. I immediately took off my seat belt to hit the roof of my car as my car was filling up with water. Do you feel that? This is what intense panic feels like. I went to open my door and I couldn't get it open, the window wasn't down and I knew if I couldn't get the door open I couldn't get out that way. I remember my passenger side window being down and then I panicked so much that my memory has blocked the part after this out. I don't remember getting out of my vehicle. I cannot, for the life of me, remember how I did. I just remember I was soaking wet, I had hay and cornfield bits all on my clothes, in my shorts and I had no idea where I was. I remember looking down at my body once I got onto the dirt road and checking myself thinking I am not alive, I didn't survive this. It was still pitch black and I couldn't see anything. I could hear lil' Wayne still blasting and I could see all the lights on my vehicle. Then, when I had a bit of hope that maybe I was okay, the music and the lights died all at once and I was legit standing in pure darkness not knowing if I was truly alive or what had just happened.

I saw some car lights coming down the road. I had no idea who it was because I had thought my friend had driven past me not knowing I crashed and completely wrecked my vehicle. This vehicle was driving slow though, so I had hope that it was her. Her first words, said with so much panic in her voice, when she pulled up beside me were, "Nicole are you okay?"

My next words were like the crazy stories where you hear a car flipping on a child and the mom gains this insane strength and lifts it off. My first words to her when I saw her were "I need to pull my car out of this ditch before my parents find out." I walked towards my vehicle and it was then I noticed I had hit a tree and that's what stopped me from rolling further. My friend pulled me back and she walked me to her passenger door and I didn't want to get in. I literally thought I could pull my vehicle out. I know how crazy that sounds but I had this belief and I had so much fear of what had just happened that I believed if I pulled my car out no one would know and I could finish my three-minute drive home and everything would be okay. If you're familiar with living in the country, the houses have green signs with just a four-digit number at the end of the person's house. Before driving away I looked at the house closest to where I had crashed and remembered the number 5892 because I was afraid we wouldn't be able to find the car again.

Yes, you read that correctly, I had about a three-minute drive left. I had to make it to three more stop signs, one left and a right and I would have pulled into my parents' driveway.

When I did pull up into my parents' driveway though this time was so different. My mom always waited up for me before she went to bed, thank god. I walked into the house and she was sitting on the couch on the phone, I shut the door and the first thing I said was don't be mad. She hung up the phone and I could hear the panic in her voice. She turned the light on and took one look at me and said "Nicole what happened?" She ran to the window and didn't see my car but what she did see was my friend parked in front of my house with her hands over her face. My mom said so sternly, "Nicole what happened and where is your car and why are you all wet?" I immediately started crying and begged her not to be mad and through the tears, I said, "Mom, I crashed my car into a ditch and hit a tree, it was filling up with water. I remember where it is though at the house marked 5892 just after their driveway on the left by the tree." She ran so fast to wake my dad up from his sleep, my cousin was living with us at the time, he was awake and my sister was in her room sleeping. This news shook everyone's world.

My mom told me to go and knock on our neighbors' door and beg him to get up and come and help us. My dad had a flatbed truck and my neighbor was a tow truck driver for the city of Toronto.

My mom, dad and I got in her car and my friend went to go get her mom and bring her to the crash site. When we pulled up to the house where I had crashed, my parents had to turn around to pull up on the other side of the road. At the time it took them to do that, there was another vehicle coming down the driveway of the house. My dad rolled down the window and I'll never forget what the man said. He said to my parents, "Did you know the girl in that vehicle?" My dad replied with a quick yes. But before my dad would get another word out. The man quickly replied, "There's no way the person made it out alive. I watched that vehicle crash from inside the house and the vehicle had to have flipped seven or eight times and the car finally stopped when they hit the tree." I burst into tears, hearing him say that when I was alive sitting in the back seat. Through the tears I opened the sliding door to the van saying to the man, "This is my vehicle sir and I crashed it but I am okay, we are going to pull it out of the ditch and go on home." He drove off, grateful that I was okay.

We waited for my neighbour to show up. The vehicle was so quiet, nothing was said. When my neighbor pulled up I remember standing with my friend, her mom and my cousin a bit away from the car. My friend's mom hugged me so tight and asked if I was okay. My cousin said, "What stupid thing did you do here now, Nicole." I started crying so hard. My neighbour who worked for the towing company came over to me and said "Nicole, I have no idea how you made it out alive from this, both your doors are pinned on either side of the ditch and I've seen vehicles and crashes like this where people don't make it out alive." I let him go back to the car and I then started to hyperventilate. I remember looking back at the tow truck lights shining on my car and when they pulled the car out and it hit the road I fell to the ground. It was at the moment my friend's mom said, "How about we bring you back to our house, get you cleaned up and get a warm hot chocolate." They got me some warm clothes and a hot chocolate. We had finished our hot chocolates and I wanted to go back home. When I arrived home the truck wasn't home yet with my vehicle, I thanked my friend and her mom for their help and walked inside. I don't remember much after this. My body was in so much shock when I sat still and alone. I started to feel a rush of anxiety come over me when I tried to comprehend what the heck just happened. I went to shower and change into some of my own clothes and I sat in the basement in my room. When I looked over my body I had one mark on my left knee cap from hitting the steering wheel when I was flipping.

The picture I would keep forever

My mom, dad and cousin arrived home. I just gave my dad a hug and he didn't say much other than, "I'm glad you're okay and it's just a car." My mom hugged me too and I told her I had worries that if I shut my eyes I wouldn't wake up because it was feeling too good to be true that I made it out alive. She replied, "Nicole, stop being so silly and go to bed." I knew they were so mad and terrified at the same time to witness what I had just survived.

So my cousin and I sat in the basement until about 5:00 am. I couldn't for the life of me shut my eyes. I was so scared. I eventually fell asleep on the couch and moved to my bed at around 7:00 am. My mom later woke me up around 9:00 am to say, "Nicole, I want you to come with me to go and look at your car that's on the flatbed." I told her I didn't want to and she replied, "You're going too because next time you may not get so lucky."

I immediately felt like I was going to be sick. We walked out to the flatbed truck with my car tarped. When my mom pulled the tarp off, I cried so hard. When I saw what I had walked away from I immediately felt so many overwhelming emotions. The vehicle was totalled, every window was smashed except my driver's side window. The passenger-side mirror was torn off, the passenger-side wheel was hanging on just barely and the roof had collapsed inwards.

The strangest part was when we got to my driver's side it was like it was untouched. The window was normal, the side mirror was on and when you tilted your head upwards inside the window there was a complete perfect circle where the roof was also untouched.

We'll come back to this but for now, I was so shocked at what I was looking at. I remember the weather was so gloomy that day. It was a grey sky overcast and it added to the eeriness of what had happened. I took a picture with my phone that I knew I would look back on and never forget this moment. I told my mom that I had to go back to the crash site and do my best to find my belongings that may have flown out the window while I flipped. My phone was one of them.

When we got back I had called my work to tell them I, unfortunately, wasn't coming in that day. When I got off the phone my mom told me that we were going to watch a video that state farm insurance had made for people to watch to learn the lesson of the outcomes from driving recklessly. It was people who were paralyzed and had other very serious consequences for their actions. I told my mom I didn't want to watch it and she told me "Nicole I know you were driving fast and next time you may not be so lucky." I know this was just her tough love and she was also terrified but I will never forget how terrified I was for my actions.

It took me about two or three weeks to even step foot into another vehicle and drive. I was told that if I didn't get over my fear I would probably never want to get back in a car again. I decided to go on a forty-five minute drive, that was the longest drive of my life and I was terrified. I drove under the speed limit. My hands were white because I was holding the steering wheel so tight and I felt like I was going to suffocate while being inside the vehicle. I also had to drive with one window down always.

I avoided that road in the future at all costs. One day, I had to drive down it as the other road was closed. I pulled over, cried and puked about three times when I got to my crash site and I had to pull over again before I got off at the end of the dirt road.

Because of my careless actions and this entire experience I can no longer listen to any of Lil' Wayne's songs, I can no longer drive on any dirt road without a window down, I cannot stand the sound of the rocks hitting the vehicle and I can't look at those little balls that flash colourful lights anymore without dealing with severe PTSD.

I promised myself that day and all those days after. Even more on the days when I struggled to get into a car, that my life was saved for reasons I could have never understood. I also shared prior to this that we lived in the country. And unfortunately, this came at the cost of many younger individuals' lives. I just want to take a moment for all the individuals this area lost during these high school years and in the years before and after, may they always rest in peace. This was one of the other hardest parts for me was that I had heard of people having accidents and not making it out of theirs. While I, the one who was so careless and reckless with my life, causes my own accident, flips my car about seven or eight times and makes it out with a bruise on my leg. I told myself there had to be a reason for this. There has to be a greater purpose to this life I'm living.

Let's just say that I have lived every day doing my best to stand by the promise that I made, to always live each day like it's your last, tell your people that you love them, give them hugs and a kiss before they leave and when they arrive. Sometimes throughout the years, I forget about this because life gets busy but there isn't a day that goes by that I don't thank my lucky stars that this careless decision didn't end my life. As the life I have created, I am so grateful, blessed that I have the opportunity and privilege to live and enjoy it and all that is still to come.

As for that picture I took of my vehicle, it has been in every vehicle I have owned up until I had my son. I am not quite ready to explain that picture to him just yet. For now, it sits in my emergency bag along with other important items in my home to hopefully one day never have another image like that again.

7

MY SOULMATE FOUND ME

Have you ever been in a place in time and your heart felt home?

I found what I never knew I was looking for

Now that you know, a bit of my story you can say my trust in anyone was very minimal. Feeling safe around men was a whole different level of comfort for me. I never had close relationships with men and I certainly wasn't looking for any such thing. But sometimes what I experienced was that life had a greater plan than I could have ever imagined.

At the high school I went to, they had a food plaza across the street so on lunch break that would pretty much be the first stop for food. I mean even though I didn't have the funds to do so, well what high school student has the funds to buy lunch every day, right? Well, this was one of those days I had eaten before because I didn't have money for food. If there was any time in my life that I was glad I didn't have lunch money that day was the day. I had sat down at a table with a friend who had bought her lunch and here came this young man whom I had never met before who sat down at the table. He sat down and said, "Hey, are you guys going to eat that bagel?" My goodness, I get butterflies even still writing this because in that exact moment he sat down I felt this moment of safety, I felt like I had known him my entire life. I felt like this was a moment where we were reunited. I know right, this sounds crazy especially because I was only fifteen years old at the time. What did most fifteen-year-olds really know anyway?

Our friendship grew over the first couple of years. We dated other people because I saw our relationship as best friends. We would see each other in the hall and chat, laugh at each other's jokes and had no real plan for anything more than that. Until grade eleven math class, when I sat down at my desk, I had no idea he was even in the same classroom until he showed up late to the class. The desks had six tables together to make one big table. I sat at one table and Andrew headed towards the same table because I and a couple others were the only people he knew. The butterflies are coming back again as I'm remembering these moments. We laughed and mainly I did my school work. Andrew still says today that I was the reason he needed summer school to pass that math class. I just laugh and think he's cute.

One math class, he came up to me and asked if I would like to go to his house for dinner and he could introduce me to his mom and dad. At the time, I didn't have my own vehicle and I couldn't drive without a licensed driver, so my mom was responsible for getting me there. I had committed the first time to the dinner but had to cancel at the last minute. It was when I canceled on him and he said he was sad I didn't make it and his mom was excited to meet me, that my heart felt like it was going to explode. This was most definitely a date that he was asking me on. So I asked him to reschedule and I was sorry for canceling. When my mom drove me to his house it was a forty-five-minute drive and we laughed at the time because tractors were driving down the road and the trees didn't even grow straight. My mom asked why I couldn't pick a guy that lives closer and we joked about at least finding someone where the trees would grow straight. Being a city girl prior to this I couldn't believe where we were driving too but again it was a place I had never been but one that also felt so familiar.

February 26th 2008 came, he had asked me to lunch but I was having a tutoring session over lunch because, let's be honest, I hated grade eleven academic math, I sucked at it but I needed a good grade to get into college. He met me just before I went into my session and he said to me, "Nicole, I asked you to go to lunch with me because I wanted to know if you would be my girlfriend?" If your teenage heart isn't beating out of your chest, I don't know if you're a real human. I, of course, said yes and he was such a gentleman and gave me a kiss on the cheek. After my math tutoring, he met me at my locker and gave me the biggest hug, picked me up off my feet and gave me the biggest kiss. His courage to ask me out would be something I would grow to be *forever* grateful for. I found my soulmate or should I say my soulmate found me, when I least expected but when I needed him most.

When we shared with people that we were dating, most people didn't even know we knew each other. On the outside, I was the one going to a math tutor during lunch and Andrew was the one skipping class and smoking cigarettes but no one felt what we felt. As corny as it sounds, I have to say my heart feels at home when I am with Andrew.

Reminded that I'm on the right path

Now, I also want to share with you that I believe in spirit guides, spiritual healers and that entire healing woowoo some may call it. I'll share this one appointment that I had with a soul reader. Now I'll also add that I had never been to one of these sessions and the lady knew only my first name. She asked me what I wanted to know, at the time I think I was eighteen or nineteen years old and I was wondering if the path I was on was the right one, you know life's greatest questions. I also wanted to know if anything was to come up for Andrew and me because we had started dating not long before this. I'll never forget this day and what she said to me. "When you first met him you knew something was different, almost like you knew him before." I replied with yes as I trembled in fear because how the heck did this woman know this. She then says "Nicole, you and Andrew have actually been Husband and Wife in another lifetime and this moment felt like that because you have reconnected with your husband from a previous lifetime." Now, keep in mind Andrew and I were still teenagers. I found comfort in her saying that because it reassured me that, yes, I was on the right path but had no big plans at this stage for a future. This voice inside always knew he was the one. Of course, I never shared that with him because hearing your girlfriend who you've only been dating for a couple years say I'm going to marry you. Yea right, could you imagine how that would make an eighteen-year-old boy feel? If that wouldn't make him run, I don't know what would. Nevermind, my friends or my family would probably think I was crazy. So, I trusted in my gut and knew it led me this far, so let's see what happens.

Trust in the journey

Within our years of dating, we did some big things together, like getting our driver's licenses and going everywhere and anywhere that wasn't home. To movie dates, camping trips, dinner dates, hockey games, dirt bike shows, snowmobile and ATV shows, going to the bars with friends and dancing the night away. Well, mainly me being the one dancing the nights away Andrew would always need a few drinks to get him on the dance floor. To epic bar fights where if someone hit on me and Andrew heard of it being the boyfriend that was so protective and kind to me, as for how kind he was to the other guy, well let's just say sorry for the other guy's luck.

The bonfires that we had with so many of our friends laughing around the fire and dancing doing what teenagers do. We build some epic memories. We both went to college and graduated and celebrated each other's big victories. We also helped each other through some of our hardest moments in our time together and had each other's back and held each other's hands through grief, loss and everything else in between.

Including the unexpected moments in our relationship where I would need Andrew the most. One night, Andrew and I had fallen asleep, his arm was on my back and his hand was touching the side of my neck. I woke up sweating, I never knew it then but I would later find out this was a time in my life where I was struggling with PTSD. I was immediately brought back to being in that stairwell and this would be the moment I would no longer be able to keep my attack to myself and I would choose to explain myself. Through the tears, I got what I could out. He was the kindest soul, even though I could imagine that he probably had so many questions. He always allowed me to share what I was comfortable with. This day would be the start of all the years ahead that he would have my back when healing through this.

We both worked through our high school years in our fields that we later went on to study in college and we both landed careers in the industries we studied. Then, one day the idea came about that we were going to move to Alberta. We thought we wanted to do it, so why not now while we're still young. We had planned to move to Alberta for a year. Go out there and see what it was all about. We had a couple of friends already out there so why not. We thought we may never get the opportunity again. We decided to tell our family and closest friends. I think most of them were pretty shocked because it came out of nowhere. I knew that we were going to do it but I was always looking for a sign, something to tell me that we were going on the right path.

The sign that showed the way

I had bought Andrew a session with a medium one year for his birthday. Keep in mind, this medium only knew our first names. Andrew's friend, who unfortunately lost his life way too soon, came through. The medium told us he was getting a message that we were thinking about making a big change in our lives. Andrew said "Yes." The medium replied, "Like a far distant change, are you think about moving?" Before we could answer he had said, "People are going to tell you not to do it and they also don't believe you're going to do it but you are." He then asked, "Are you planning on moving to Alberta?" Andrew and I couldn't look at each other fast enough with such shock as to what we were hearing. Andrew replied with "Yes." The medium said, "This is going to be your home, where you plant your roots and it's going to happen, it's actually already happening." We left with so many other incredible messages but if that wasn't the massive sign that we were doing this big move, I don't know what else could beat that.

We were terrified, had no plan, no jobs, just our life packed up in an 06 dodge ram pick up with a U-Haul trailer in tow with all of our belongings except the kitchen sink. Like I kid you not, we had a dirt bike, a pet gecko in the back seat that we had to change the heating pads under the sand every eight hours. It's funny sometimes because I think back now and I am so proud of our younger selves for making the choice and the decision that we made because so many things could have gone wrong but when a heart decides and a mind is made, it's going to happen and whatever you want to happen will come true. We focused on getting to Calgary and spoke about how excited we were to get there and yes it was heart-wrenching to leave *everything* we knew. Our safe places, our parents, our friends and families, our homes and everything else that was familiar to us for the hope and tug in our bellies that we were meant to move to Alberta.

The farewells that led to our greatest adventure

I have to tell you I will always remember September 29th, 2014 as it was the day we had to pull away and leave my parents, my sister, my childhood home that I grew to love. The farewells were heart-wrenching. I had to get Andrew to pull over three times because I was sick to my stomach as I am such a family person. Before this, the longest time I had *ever* been away from my parents was no longer than a week's time. Life is pretty interesting isn't it, the place that I hated years ago before we even set foot in, this town called Beeton, I was heartbroken to leave. Then it was time where we had to say farewell to Andrew's family and I never met anyone similar to me on an emotional level until I met Andrew's mom. This was just as heart-wrenching for Andrew to say goodbye as it was for me to watch it. This day was one of the hardest moments that we had yet to go through but we did it.

There was nothing but tears in our eyes for the first while and then when we got away from everything we knew, we focused on the open road for the next three days. We had no idea what we would come across and had nothing but faith in our hearts that things would turn out okay.

Little did we know at the time our greatest adventure yet was going to be unfolded.

8

OUR ROOTS ARE PLANTED

Have you ever experienced a moment in life where it was better than you could have ever envisioned?

To say that only happened to me once would be a lie.

Calgary, Alberta Adventure

When we arrived in Calgary, Alberta, I had never felt more out of place and more at home at the same moment in time. Something felt so right. We were planning on crashing with a couple of our friends until we could get on our own feet. Andrew scored a job in a short time while I on the other hand, well, I was three months into searching for a job. I was told I knew too much in my field and if the person was to hire me they would be afraid I would know more than them. I never felt so frustrated and mad at the knowledge I had. It took three full months until I found something and it was the last place I had applied to. I knew this last place felt like the place I would work. I don't know why I get these feelings but when I get them I just follow them. It was about a week after I handed in my resume and I hadn't heard anything back about if I was hired or not so I called time and time again until I landed myself an interview and guess what, sometimes you've got to just go for what you want and not wait for anyone else. I was told I got the job because of my eagerness to follow up. It was a medical aesthetics job and I was thrilled because it was two blocks walking distance from our house. Because of course, moving across Canada I left my car in Ontario. So we were set up. A place to live and the two of us had great jobs.

Then my sister and her boyfriend showed up to join the Alberta Family and they did the same as us, found jobs and made this place their home. Our friend's place ended up being our living situation for one year and my goodness I didn't do residence in college but this living arrangement made up for that. The stories we made here are even wilder than some movies I've seen.

At the end of the day, these people here are solid as a rock when it comes to family! Andrew and I were just missing a fur baby, so we added our miniature pinscher pup named Gizmo to the family and he made everything so much better.

We, of course, did all the touristy things and fell in love with this province. I bought my first dirt bike and to say the adventures have been a wild ride would be an understatement, to say the least.

We moved into another house in Calgary that again, felt so perfect, so much that the four of us, Andrew, my sister and her boyfriend all moved in together again. We loved this house. It was massive inside and had a massive backyard. We actually all ended up living together again with our original starting Alberta family. The nights we all shared living life to the fullest, I'll just add our livers hated us but the stories were golden.

We partied and lived life up huge, we went to the bars, we went to all the country concerts, the Calgary Stampede did a number on our bodies along with our bank accounts.

We did some other things we had never done before, like attending a big brother big sister bowling charity event and I remember the moment we drove into the town, I told Andrew we were going to live there one day. All I knew was the name of the town, Cochrane, Alberta.

Andrew and I had spoken about buying a house and yes we stopped going to the bars and spending unnecessary money on things we didn't really need to start saving for our down payment. Little did we know life had a greater plan for the timing of when that would be.

With all the fun we were having Andrew and I were not feeling any younger. We went for a drive one day to find a dirt bike trail and we never did find that trail but instead of the trail, we found the houses my sister's boyfriend built and he was so excited to show us in this community in Cochrane.

A couple hours later, we walked out with home building plans and had twenty-four hours to get our deposit for our lot.

Building our first home together

Building our first home was such a life-changing excitement. I will never forget how terrified and unsure we were at this stage in our life. We just focused on the final home we were going to have because of all this hard work and took each step one at a time. Let me tell you something though, this was very challenging at times because we had never done this before and it didn't take long for the thoughts of fear and worry of what we just did to sink in. But hey, focusing on the end goal and shushing everything else seemed to work to get us to this point so far.

It was so fun picking out everything custom for our home. Overwhelming at times because there were so many appointments to schedule for the entire process. From the flooring choices to the paint colours. The style and pulling everything together to custom make our kitchen. To the bathrooms, the electrical placements, ceiling fans, doors, trim and so many other choices for everything else that would make up our home. It was so much fun and we learned so much along the way.

In December 2015, we had the final walk-through that we scheduled at Christmas time so my family could be part of it as well. It was so magical. I'll be totally honest at this time in my life it was very hard for me to imagine what everything would look like completed.

At the end of January 2016, we finally got the keys to our beautiful, brand new home that had all our choices that pulled together so beautifully with the finishing touches. I was so emotional when we first moved in. I couldn't believe this home was ours. We had worked so hard for so long and it was a moment in our life that I will remember forever.

It's about to be a bumpy ride

If you've read the other book I was so grateful to be part of called Lead with Love, I shared my motherhood journey in there but for those who haven't heard my journey to being a mom, hold on to your hats, it's a bumpy ride.

We decided we were going to try for a baby. We were in Newfoundland for my parents' twenty-fifth wedding renewal and I was so sick the entire time. I totally thought it was that I ate too many different foods than what I usually would. Until we arrived back from Newfoundland to Calgary to find out that I was pregnant in July of 2016. I was so excited. We told so many people because we were so excited about this new chapter in our life. My friend and I planned a surprise photoshoot to be taken of us riding our dirt bikes. Thank god Andrew's bike wouldn't start that day because I wouldn't have been riding mine anyways. I remember Andrew being so mad that he couldn't bring his bike. During the photoshoot, Andrew and I stood back to back and we both wrote something we loved about each other. I cannot for the life of me remember what he wrote but when he turned around mine read "You're going to be a dad." I had this bright green box that had toddler dirt bike gloves with a note that read you'll soon welcome me to be the newest part of our dirt bike team. This time in our life was filled with so much happiness. Until August 19 2016 when we, unfortunately, lost our baby to a miscarriage.

After that loss it was heartbreaking and I needed a while to comprehend what just happened and deal with the grief along with sharing what had happened with our family.

Throughout the heartbreak, Andrew was always there like a brick house of strength.

I also think it was from experiencing that loss how much we knew we truly wanted a baby and wanted to be with each other for the rest of our lives. I mean it was eight years of us dating by this point. I always knew I would marry him, just wasn't sure of when.

We'd be together forever

Andrew came home one night in October 2016. He was nervous and acting weird. I had torn a chest muscle that night and needed to get some rest. I'll never forget this night because Andrew was wandering around the house like someone who had somewhere to go but wasn't sure where he was going. I didn't think anything of it, and the next day he stayed home with me.

He then asked me if I wanted to go down to the river for a walk. I was like, not really babe, my chest is killing me. He made a good point though and said, "It would be fun to get out and stretch our legs." So here we go getting ready for our walk by the river.

Andrew threw rocks at the river and our dog was going crazy at the time, I'm walking down the river with our pup and I heard Andrew call my name from behind me. When I turned around there he was, on one knee. I couldn't believe my eyes. I of course cried and eventually replied with a yes!!!

We celebrated huge with this new chapter. I loved calling Andrew my fiance.

We also made other big life changes shortly after Andrew proposed. We got our second dog Rocko. He was the tiniest pup I ever saw. He could fit in my hand when we got him. We wanted to get another dog to take away some of our baby fever. That and we lived with so many people for so long we thought, let's enjoy our quiet time and caring for a pup would help and we'd consider trying for a baby when it felt right. Snuggling and watching a puppy grow sure did help a lot though.

Pregnancy number two

We decided to try again for another baby during this time. February of 2017 came and I was sitting at home with a pregnancy test. I couldn't believe I was here again. I never wanted something so bad but was also so unsure of my strength. I gave the test the usual three minutes, which were the longest three minutes of my life. I flipped that test over and it showed that yes, I was most definitely pregnant. We were going to have a baby again. This pregnancy felt different.

I wanted to surprise Andrew when I told him and I went to a donut shop and picked up six donuts where I put a note inside that read, mommy can't be the only fat one this summer, eat up daddy! I recorded the video and I was so nervous to tell him but of course, I was going to. I couldn't believe that I got the opportunity to tell Andrew again that he was going to be a dad. Let's just say we held in the excitement this time. As we learned our lesson the first time. We only told our parents and our siblings. We told them by holding up a Christmas bulb that said, Grandpa and Grandma. It was such an emotional time in our life.

We made it to our first pregnancy appointment at the OBGYN office. When I first got there and stepped on the scale, the nurse pointed out that I wasn't gaining weight. We went back to the room and while the nurse did the exam she couldn't successfully hear the heartbeat. I immediately felt sick and started to cry as I put my clothes back on. I told Andrew that it was happening again and something was wrong. He looked me straight in the eyes and said that we just had to wait to be sure. When the nurse came back into the room, she mentioned we had an urgent ultrasound booked next door. Working in a doctors office I, unfortunately, knew too much, I knew that when there was a scan booked that fast something wasn't right. We went next door and as they were doing the scan I felt extremely sick. We were told to wait until the radiologists came in to tell us the results. The person came into the room and said there was no blood flow and they couldn't see a heartbeat. The radiologist added that the baby hadn't progressed past nine weeks. I was thirteen weeks and a bit into my pregnancy. Later on, it was unsure if everything was okay or not as I stopped bleeding then started again. My family doctor booked us in for another repeat scan to be sure as to what was going on. This technician was the kindest I had ever met, she took the time to show us everything on the screen and show that unfortunately there was no blood flow. Little did I know I would go through three weeks of uncertainty before I experienced another loss of another baby.

This one was so tragic compared to the first one. The first one I passed in the toilet at home, which yes, in its own ways, was very tragic. But my second loss was like nothing I had experienced to date. I was in such a high intensity of pain. I had back pain that woke me up right out of my sleep. I couldn't take the pain anymore and my fiance asked what we should do. I told him he either had to call an ambulance or get me to the emergency as fast as he could. So we got ready as fast as we could. I could barely walk down the stairs because of the pain and I needed a freshly boiled heating pad on my back to make the slightest difference in the pain relief. I had to breathe through the waves of pain that came every few minutes.

When we got to the hospital I had to go in alone while my fiance parked. When I stepped out of the car I felt a huge gush, I thought it was either my water breaking or I had just had another miscarriage. I sat down in the triage and I started to hyperventilate as I knew what was happening or what was coming. I told the nurse I was having or had just had another miscarriage, she told me to calm down and she would get me to be seen right away. She was right, Andrew didn't arrive back from parking the car and she was already wheeling me back with a nurse and a specialist from gynecology. I told them I wasn't going anywhere without my fiance as I was deathly allergic to penicillin and I forgot my medical bracelet. He made it back before they were wheeling me away. We went back to the room and they wouldn't let him in with me. All I wanted was for him to hold my hand. The doctor did a pelvic check and confirmed that everything was sitting in the opening of the cervix and it needed to be removed. I told him I needed someone to hold my hand and if my fiance could be the one, that would be great. A second later, a nurse walked in. The doctor advised me that it would be my body's normal reflex to sit up when he tugged on everything and for me to do my best to stay still. He tugged and sure enough, straight up I went. The pain was like nothing else. He didn't have enough time to cover everything so unfortunately, I saw everything. My baby that I was so excited for, had now been passed and removed in a matter of seconds. I told them I needed to see my fiance immediately.

When he walked in I was crying so hard. I had to be strong and pull through the tears and tell him what had just happened. He was heartbroken and in shock. We had to stay for a while after because my body wouldn't stop bleeding. After about forty-five minutes of waiting another gynecologist came into the room. For me to tell her the above story and for her to be paged to delivery. So we waited about another hour and a half. I was advised that the nurse had to put on a blood transfusion bracelet depending on how much blood I had lost or if I had to go for surgery they were prepared. Finally, the gynecologist came back to do an exam and she had found remnants still inside. So if going through that entire experience the first time wasn't enough, here was the second time. Andrew held my hand and I cried so hard. She told me she was done and in forty-five minutes I should stop bleeding and could go home.

Forty-five minutes later, I stopped bleeding and unfortunately, I had gone through all that pain to be told to go home while my hands, belly and heart were empty. The healing I would later have to face because of this time in my life is heart-wrenching and to say I will be healed from either of these experiences is untruthful. I think this will take my lifetime. But I needed to believe there was a greater plan for our parenting journey. With the slightest bit of hope and some days, barely any, I survived. There was lots of darkness and tears but through it all, I continued to put one foot in front of the other and believed something good had to come from all this heartache.

Our wedding and honeymoon

Planning our wedding and honeymoon was such a well-needed distraction from trying for a baby. It was such a fun and exciting time for us. We found the perfect venue when one of my dearest friends showed me a picture from her wedding held there. It was a barn-like structure with a massive fire pit in the middle of the room with the center of the roof removed, they actually called this building the donut for that reason. I loved this venue as I immediately envisioned us dancing under the stars by the fire and surrounded by mountains and the Bow River and all our closest loved ones. Doesn't that sound so dreamy or what?

I was so excited to get married but parts of me were sad because I always envisioned that we would have a baby at our wedding. The fact that we were coming up to our wedding and didn't have a baby made all kinds of feelings come up for me. I remember the night before our wedding I was showering and I immediately sobbed. I couldn't believe I didn't have any of those babies I got so excited for with us on this special day. I felt this deep part of me missing on our special day.

Once I worked through these emotions and had some conversations to help me through the excitement about the life I was currently living, bringing myself into the present moment was what got me through. Which reminded me that I was so excited to finally marry my high school sweetheart.

Our wedding day was the most magical day we had experienced to date. The butterflies all came back in full swing before I was to walk down the aisle with my dad surrounded by all our closest family and friends.

Our two hearts had become one on this very special day. We had the beautiful mountains, the river and all our special people there to witness our love becoming one. These loved ones watched as Andrew and I promised each other eternity.

Shortly after our wedding, we went on our honeymoon, we traveled to Vancouver, British Columbia and Vancouver Island. This was a time where we had no plan but open roads and whatever we wanted to do that day we did. It was the most freeing time I had ever experienced and the special moments would be cherished for our entire lifetime. It was crazy to me because we had been together for ten years already but still hadn't done so many things. Like traveling to BC, taking a ferry together, a seaplane tour, a whale watching tour, visiting our first ever castle, living out of an SUV and so many other special memories were made during this honeymoon.

Our greatest gift

When we came back from our honeymoon, I was three weeks late for my cycle and I couldn't bring myself to do a test. I was terrified at the fact that I could be pregnant and I didn't want to get my hopes up again at the possibility of becoming a mom. But like I shared with you a couple times previous to this, life has a greater plan than we could ever imagine sometimes. I previously shared that we always wanted to have a baby with us on our wedding day and little did we know, we received everything we had ever wanted to this point.

I share all of these memories and times in my life from our journey in Alberta because yes, it would have been so easy to be terrified and turn that truck around when we had all our belongings in the back of that dodge pickup. Let fear and worry overcome us and get caught up in how each next step was going to happen and really become paralyzed by the how. But, my friend, trust me when I say this, sometimes, you just have to go for everything you've ever wanted no matter how much time it takes or how many times you have to get up after being knocked down. It is in the moments when you keep going that you will be so proud of what you can accomplish. All that will come your way could be way better than you could EVER imagine. The province of Alberta, at one time such a strange place, would be my forever home. All the greatest things in my life have come from this adventure. I learned to trust in the unknown, believe in myself and even despite others' uncertainty and worries to trust in my intuition.

Let's be honest that intuition of mine has guided me pretty well up to this point. From the deepest part of my heart, I want to share that finding this man Andrew all those years ago, not for a moment knowing what life would bring us. I have currently grown to love him for forteen years and he has become my best friend, husband, soulmate, high school sweetheart, the father of our child and the one who always has my back. He saved me at a time that I didn't realize I needed to be saved. During the time I had no idea I was looking for him when I found him. The life we share today I used to dream of when I was a small child and I feel like I have to pinch myself sometimes. I am so grateful for our paths crossing, for the incredible life we have built today along with our beautiful family that led us to be called The Recker's.

9

MY GREATEST GIFT

Throughout this journey of becoming a momma, I've had difficult obstacles, lots of fear, and uncertainty. But I've also learned so much.

Hold the faith

Yes, of course, it would have been easy to give up on having a family. Still, with this pregnancy after our wedding and honeymoon, I let myself feel what I wanted to feel. Some days that looked like doing nothing but crying and going down to the river to throw some rocks to blow off some steam. While other days it was me holding and loving my belly through all the upcoming stages for every day I was pregnant. Every single day I woke up and decided to feed my mind faith, truth, and a whole lot of love. Your mind only knows what you feed it.

The hardest part was accepting that I had no control over my situation. It didn't matter how much I wanted it. I couldn't choose the outcome. No matter what, I had to let what was going to happen. And I did just that, and my goodness, I am so grateful I did because I was soon to be gifted with another part of life's greater plan.

I believe my journey to becoming a mom made me a stronger being as a whole. I continued to remind myself that I owed it to myself to keep trying because the weight of regret was something I was never willing to live with. My intuition kept telling me to keep going and not give up. I trusted it so deeply. Hope. Faith. Resilience. Persistence. Never give up. These are the words that got me through the next part of my life.

Never give up

I decided to surprise my husband. I told him that we would go down to the river to take a picture. I told him I would write "fall in love" on a chalkboard and take a picture.

There we were, at the river, the exact spot he had proposed. I set up the video camera and hit record. I walked back to him with the chalkboard hidden. I turned it around, and it read, "You're going to be a dad." He looked at me with tears in his eyes, his voice cracking, and asked, "Really?"

I booked our first appointment at the doctor's and cried when I heard her say, "Nicole, you're pregnant."

We arrived at our eight-week ultrasound, and I was a nervous wreck. The technician said, "You've got a healthy baby there. Everything looks great." I cried so hard in relief. We left feeling so grateful.

Gratitude

Be like a Buffalo.

These were the wise words that my Midwife shared as I came closer to the end of my pregnancy.

This pregnancy was a complete fairy tale. I remember hearing our baby's heartbeat for the first time and crying tears of joy every time I had the opportunity to listen to it. I recorded every single one.

As my body grew, I looked at myself in the mirror differently. My heart was filled with gratitude for all the special moments I had gone through. The ones I was soaking up in the present and the future moments to come—even the ones where I wanted to puke at the smell of taco meat cooking.

I hugged my belly, spoke, and sang to my baby. I drank something sweet to feel my baby move around. I enjoyed the feeling of movement when my baby would stretch and kick me in the ribs. The best was when I was sleeping, and my husband would have his arm across my belly, and our baby would wake us both up with a kick that would move my husband's arm. I enjoyed feeling everything. So much so that I decided I wanted to have a natural delivery. I wanted to experience it all; after all, I never knew if I'd get this experience again.

Of course, fear and negative thoughts tried to sneak in during my delivery, but I knew they weren't serving me. I had doubts, and for split seconds, I wanted to give up during delivery, but I reminded myself that I had gone through worse to receive less. This pain was a good thing as I knew these pains meant I was going to meet my baby and I knew the best was yet to come. I used the power of meditation, motivational quotes, and breathing through all the hard stuff. I never lost sight of the goal.

I was finally going to have my family.

Inner strength

I learned that we have to surrender and stop fighting against the challenges and instead rise to them as they were made to make us better. You see, sometimes the biggest gift in this lifetime is on the other side of all of the heartbreak. All the uncertainty, all the unanswered questions, and all the pain.

It was worth it for me, and I would do it all over again, knowing I would hold my little man at the end. I am forever grateful that I chose never to give up and continued to have hope. The best thing that ever happened to me, besides my husband, was having my son.

I got what I always wanted, my family. I successfully had my son naturally. The inner strength I never knew I had, was found. I did it. Wow, I beat it all. I chose to never give up, and this was my victory moment.

With this victory moment, I met someone I knew nothing about.

The new me I was becoming. I learned so much about myself in the three days after having him than I did in my entire life. People ask me what the biggest thing I learned when I became a mom was.

Patience.

Patience to get things done in a different order than what I had in mind.

I had patience with myself to heal when I was ready, not when I wanted to be ready.

Patience with this little human who had just been birthed to an entirely new world. He needed the most patience and love that I never knew existed.

The love between a momma and child is the most instant love I have ever felt. That exact moment he squirmed right up to me, and I looked right into his eyes, and he looked back at me. Immediately a love surfaced bigger than I ever knew possible. My entire world is complete with my Family.

Caring for my son, seeing him smile for the very first time. Hearing all of his little sounds, learning all of his cues, all of his different cries. Learning through all of the new stages. Hearing him call momma and dada. Having him run around with my husband and hearing them laughing those incredible belly laughs together. Hearing his voice. Watching him make sense of this world we live in along with our incredible conversations and a million other things is truly so rewarding.

Rebirth

I find comfort knowing the babies from my previous pregnancies have been reborn with my son.

Which to some may sound a little woo woo.

But, hear me out. Some things you just can't explain.

My first loss was on August 20, 2016.

My second loss was on April 19, 2017.

Wyatt was born in the year 2019.

I choose to believe that the dates I lost those other babies, 20th and 19th, were no coincidence that Wyatt was born in 2019.

Despite feeling like I have the entire world with my family, being a mom has its challenges. Mine tend to come with mental challenges where I fight two people in my head. The one part of my brain, the mom, the me who gave it my all to hold it together still to feel like I didn't do enough. While the other part of me reminds myself never to complain, as there was a time in my life when I would truly give anything to have what I have today.

I'm going to share some personal stories that allow a glimpse into my world with my handsome little man. This one reminded me again that if you wait long enough, life will show you the greatest plan you could have ever imagined for your life.

The greater plan continues

One afternoon, my heart overflowed so much that I cried on our drive back from our adventure. Why?

Because I have a massive grateful heart for this little man.

We are a very loving family. We hug, say I love you, and give kisses all the time. We express ourselves and have the longest conversations even though when my son was younger, I couldn't always understand the words. We tell him powerful messages, teach him positivity, self-worth, confidence, strong beliefs in himself, and to love wholeheartedly.

On that drive home, I told him how I was so proud of him because he did such a good job on our adventure. He said please and thank you without being asked, he got in his seat without a meltdown, and he listened so well the entire time. As I was looking back at him in my rearview mirror, I paused for a moment and said, "I love you so much, baby."

He looked back at me in the mirror and said, "I love you, momma."

My heart exploded, and tears rolled down my cheeks. When I was pregnant, I would wonder how his voice would sound, and my goodness, I struck gold with him.

I would go on to record everything, take so many pictures to cherish all of these moments I waited years for, and here are some I'll share with you.

Raising my son Wyatt I will add that I am all about showing, communicating, and speaking to him like a real human. Explaining things that someone else may not make the time for or some things I do, someone else may not agree with, but I love parenting because we all have our own individual ways. I also strived to show my son compassion, empathy, kindness, and strength even when we may not feel like it and to express ourselves whenever we want. To remind him that he has a voice, it matters, and knowing that he will change the world.

The moments he won't remember but I will never forget

I also have learned, which has been a journey for me, that it is so important for Wyatt to see me expressing all of the emotions. As earlier in my motherhood journey, I would hide when I was crying because he was so emotionally connected to me. I learned that if he couldn't see me regulate my emotions and feel everything, he wouldn't learn how. This one day was an emotional day for me after having a breakdown about life. Wyatt being the kindest soul, kept hugging me and just being with me the entire time. I said to him after I stopped crying that I was thankful that he is always being there for momma when I was feeling sad. His reply, "I'm always here momma."

I have also always taught Wyatt to use his manners and say please and thank you all the time. Another thing that we say a lot is that we love each other. One day Wyatt and I were lying down for a nap, and Wyatt said, "Momma, I love you more than much, giant much." Before I could tell Andrew, it was now bedtime, and Andrew was leaving the room, and Wyatt said, "I love you dada, giant much!" This has become his go-to way to say I love you. I remember my husband texting me immediately after, and saying that warmed my heart so much.

It blows my mind that he understands that things like the mountains are giants, dinosaurs are giant, and the distance between things can be giant. To have his mind comprehend that and add in giant much at the end of every love you, my goodness, he knows how to melt my entire heart.

He continues to do so with all the things he says. October 17th was a big day for him, saying cute things. Along with a massive day for Wyatt. I asked Wyatt what he wanted for Christmas, and I have no idea where he learnt this, but his reply was priceless. He said, "Momma, a white Christmas." I went on to tell him that I was so proud of him, and I asked him if he was proud of himself. (We, as a family, ask him if he's proud of himself versus only telling him we're proud of him. So he grows up knowing that it's a good thing to be proud of himself versus needing validation from others to be proud of himself in order to feel good.) His reply was, "I'm so proud of me, and I'm so proud of you." He quickly asks, "Are you proud of yourself, momma?"

While Wyatt is learning to potty train, we are using the sticker method to encourage him to love the experience. When he uses the potty, he gets to choose a sticker, along with when he brushes his teeth, he also gets to choose a sticker. I share this with you because my husband decided to quit smoking. So every day within the first while, Wyatt would ask Andrew how he did today and when Andrew would reply with no smoking today. Wyatt would run for his sticker and say, "Good job dada, I'm so proud of you; you get to choose a sticker." Let's just say my husband went to sleep with a lot of stickers on his hands. But the thoughtfulness in Wyatt's actions had warmed our hearts.

Including moments if any of us have to go to any form of appointment. Wyatt will say to whoever is going, be brave, be strong, you're kind, you're going to change the world. He will even say this to my oldest dog, who goes to the vet every month before he goes to remind him of all of those things.

Wyatt also loves nature shows or anything educational, along with reading all kinds of books. Shortly after Wyatt turned two, he memorized three entire books, and he would always shush either my husband or I if we tried to read any of the pages that he knew. One night we were reading a book, and he said to me after seeing a salmon in a book. He says, "Momma, that's a big fish that swims upstream. They were all gone, and then they got big and went back up the river." I said, honey are you talking about the bear that looks for salmon, where there were none in the water, then the salmon swam upstream and the bear found them. He replies, "Yea, momma, the salmon are so big and the bears are so happy." Here he's referring to a national geographic documentary about bears.

One day we were lying down for his nap, and he said to me, "Momma, with wolves, you be brave and strong and don't be scared." He then said, "Momma, you know sharks swim in the water, and they eat and swim after fish."

Sharing earlier that I want Wyatt to be able to express himself whenever he wants. One day we came home from meeting his little cousin for the very first time, and of course, I cried when meeting him. He sits down once we arrive home and says, "Momma, I'm sad." I replied, "Why, Hunny?" He said, "I'm sad like momma was with Mason." I explained to him that those were mommas happy tears, as I was so happy to meet Mason, and that's why I cried. He then states in such a proud voice, "Momma, I am so happy, I cry too."

Wyatt also has a massive love for animals. Including our two small pups. This also shows you just a small look into his incredible personality. Wyatt is playing with our youngest pup, Rocko, and Wyatt says, "Momma, Rocko licks me like I lick ice cream!" I laughed so hard.

This one night will be another one that I cherish so deeply. Wyatt and I were lying in bed reading some stories, and this was our conversation.

Me: Wyatt, I love you so much!

Wyatt: Why momma?

Me: Because you're the greatest gift I have ever received.

Wyatt: No, momma, you're the greatest gift I ever received.

Me: Wyatt, you're the best

Wyatt: No, momma, you're the best.

Me: Uncontrollably crying

I immediately cried because I thought, I can't believe I almost gave up on having him. It is these magical moments like this and all of these above memories I shared with you and so many more why I AM FOREVER GRATEFUL TO MY YOUNGER SELF. Even though I was terrified and had no idea what was to come. I AM FOREVER GRATEFUL that my husband and I choose to never give up and keep going anyways.

The full circle moment

December 13, 2021, was the day after I decided to publish this very book. Like I shared above about the story of being like a buffalo. The words that came out of my son's mouth next warmed my entire being. I don't believe in coincidences; this day, I was questioning and wondering if the choice I had made to publish this book was the right one. Let's be real for a moment; fear of what others would think tried to sneak in and consume my brain, and I said to myself, "Snap out of it, Nicole. Remember the reasons you're doing this. It's way bigger than me." And then, Wyatt says these words out of nowhere, and he couldn't have said them at a better time.

Wyatt: Momma, you're a buffalo.

Me: Why am I a buffalo baby?

Wyatt: Because you're brave, momma.

Me: Aww, Wyatt, you're the best.

Wyatt: I'm a small and tiny buffalo momma.

Me: Yes, Hunny.

Wyatt: Yes, I'm a small and tiny buffalo because I'm brave too.

Me: Yes, Wyatt, you are very brave. We will be buffaloes together. (As my heart explodes in pure joy)

I know there will be a million and one of these moments that I will continue to write down and find one day. I will be reminded of these moments that he will never remember and ones I will never forget. This little human being named Wyatt has taught me and will continue to guide me and show me the way for all the years to come. He will be a constant reminder of how much unimaginable strength one can have. Along with how much a child can create a space to reflect on how one can choose to show up differently. Children are like mirrors; they reflect exactly what they see. In other words, they are great imitators, and I will work my butt off to be sure that he has something great to imitate. A child will show someone where they may need to grow and learn new ways to be different while raising a child. Which was and is always a reminder in some situations I can be in control during this journey.

I know this journey of motherhood will last my entire lifetime and long after I am gone from this earth. I hope my little man Wyatt, even when he's not so little, continues to know that his voice matters, his story matters. I wish for him to know that being kind is always the best way, that he is courageous, strong, and to always say please and thank you. While knowing deep down that he will change the world in a big way because of his greatness. Most importantly, I hope he remembers that his dad and I love him more than all the stars in the sky, the fish in the sea, trees in the forest, and water in the oceans.

I look forward to all the moments ahead with the family I've dreamed of and the family that I am so lucky to have.

10

GRIEF SHOWS UP IN THE MOST UNEXPECTED TIMES

Losing a baby in pregnancy is something I am familiar with, but the grief that continues to arise is unknown territory for me. Yes, I get the most grateful privilege of living this lifetime with my husband and our precious little man. But to be honest, I still have moments of grief while raising him. I still have my days and constant reminders of the babies that came before him.

This is a level of grief that no one can prepare you for. The suffering that sneaks in with the slightest things. Shopping at the grocery store and walking past the baby clothes. Standing next to a person at the grocery store and her little one is crying, and she looks over, to say to me, "Have kids" they said, "It would be so fun". I had attended a friend's baby shower when I was supposed to be pregnant, too, while smiling and holding myself together, all in the same second. Riding a bike and ever wonder if I'd hear a little wee sound coming from a little human. Babysitting a friend's child and wondering if I'd ever get to experience those moments with my own baby. Having friends who would say, "Oh, I didn't even have to try to get pregnant, I could just think about getting pregnant, and it happened."

This is grief no one can prepare you for.

Sometimes what triggers this type of grief is different every single day.

One of my unexpected trigger moments was when we were decorating our Christmas tree. Decorating a Christmas tree is such a happy time of year for most. My family and I started taking ornaments out of our storage bin. Christmas music played in the background, and we danced around with Santa and elf hats on. Wyatt was hanging up some decorations with Andrew, and I completely forgot about these three ornaments inside our bin. See, sometimes I try to forget the parts of me that hurt the most, and it's something like these ornaments that rock my world and make me fall apart.

I pulled the first one out; it was a circular yellow ornament with 'Someone we love was never born' with the dates of our two losses written on it. I immediately felt my tears coming on. But I also didn't want to cry in the video we were making. So I held it together.

The second ornament that I found was given to me for the losses of my two babies and for our other family members that we lost too soon. This ornament was circular with a silver speckle to it, and it had written on it 'Because someone we love is in heaven there's a little bit of heaven in our home'.

The third ornament, to some, may seem so pointless, but it was a wooden cut out of a little silver bird. Well, this was the ornament that I chose during Christmas of 2018. I was pregnant with Wyatt. Andrew, my sister, and I had gone to a candlelight ceremony at the children's hospital for people who had infant or pregnancy losses. They had a candle along with a Christmas ornament that you could take and put on the tree they had on display.

If you can believe it, when we were decorating the tree, I NEVER cried.

After I was all alone at the kitchen sink, I downloaded a video my dearest best friend had worked so hard to make of Wyatt's entire first year. She had made an hour and a bit long video for us to watch. Once it stopped downloading, the video just randomly started playing. The first clip was of me telling Andrew he was going to be a dad during my pregnancy with Wyatt.

The waterworks were finally released.

Be kind to yourself

I understand that yes, I, the one who has a healthy baby boy with so many incredible memories that I am forever grateful to make but I still grieve the losses of my babies that came many years before him. There doesn't have to be a timeline of when we should "feel okay."

My biggest lesson is to be kind to yourself. The fact that no one can prepare you for this is a greater reason for you to be kind to yourself. This is a path never traveled before. It can be dark, scary, roller coaster up and down feels and sometimes even like you're personally being attacked. But no one knows this path that you're walking. Only you. So be kind, and trust me, your future self will be so proud of you for doing so.

As for other people possibly not knowing the path you're on, do yourself the honor of sharing your story, no matter what. It may take your courage to do so, that will allow room for someone else to do the same.

So to anyone reading this that is going through a hard time. I see you! I love you! You are appreciated! You've got this, and keep going!

11

THE SPIRITS THAT GUIDED ME HOME

The spirits I thought were scary movie-level spirits were the ones that guided me home and allowed me to understand that I had a greater purpose.

I have been someone who has grown up with spirits. Some of the stories I'll share, still make my hairs stand up on the back of my neck. So if you're afraid of this type of stuff, maybe this is a chapter you skip over, or maybe you read closer to the bottom because there's a reason for sharing these with you.

A glimpse into my world with spirits

When I was small, I would hear things, and I would also see things. I lived in Scarborough, Ontario, Canada, with my mom, dad, and sister. I share that so you know that when I share these stories, no other people could have made any of these things happen for those of you who are massive disbelievers about this topic. I will also share that my role in sharing these stories isn't to convince anyone. I just recommend you do your best to make it to the end of the chapter to find out what happens.

There were always things that happened that had no explanation. I remember all of these stories like they happened yesterday, probably because I was so terrified. It will also explain why I don't watch scary movies.

The unexplained

I remember one night as I was sleeping, and I could feel the presence of something staring at me. When I looked in my doorway, I saw a full black shadow staring into my bedroom. I remember immediately pulling the covers over my head and saying it's not real and it can't hurt me until I eventually fell asleep.

My sister would always say that she could see a little girl with red hair playing. I, on the other hand, never really saw anything other than the black shadow.

My mom was home by herself while my dad, sister, and I were visiting our family in Newfoundland. My mom called my dad scared because she could hear someone in our back shed. She said the lights were on, and all the tools were going off inside the shed. My dad told her to call 911. She sat under the window so that the person wouldn't be able to see her inside the home. When she started to dial 911, every noise stopped, and the shed went black. This is one of the stories that still makes my hair stand up. Scary feeling, right.

I remember some other stories in between while staying at this home. Still, that last story made my mom look into getting a medium to pass over the spirits so we wouldn't be experiencing these things anymore. The medium told her that she couldn't come as they haven't completed done what they needed to do. So the medium told her to tell the spirits to leave as they weren't welcome anymore.

Our new home and they found us again

When my family moved to our other home in the country, it wasn't right away that we would experience things, but they eventually started happening there too. Things would be moved; one person would walk into the room and say there's an item on the table, and the next person would go, and it wouldn't be there.

I'll never forget the moment when my family was hanging out in the basement watching a family movie. I can laugh about it now, but at the time, it was terrifying. We would hear people running around upstairs, and we lived in a bungalow with no one else in the home. My dad, to say the least, hated talking about these stories. When this happened, he told my sister and me that it was probably just our dog. For us to respond with, "Ugh, Princess is sitting right beside us, dad." He was so terrified that he told my mom to go upstairs to check. She came back downstairs and said nothing was upstairs. We all finished watching the movie, and I remember sleeping upstairs that night.

We would tell these stories to some people we knew, and they would always just say, "Yeah, right." Until some of them experienced them on their own. I remember my dad said he had some people over to help him put some flooring in our basement. He said they had heard noises upstairs of people running around when no one was home and told us that they finally believed us and left when we arrived.

Things would go missing and return

We would also have things go missing and return in the most strange ways. For example, my mom and I had gone to a town baseball game, and we had lost her cell phone at the game. My friend and I had used her cell phone to call my mom's phone. Someone picked up, and it was the strangest monotone man who answered. She said, "Um, this is my friend's mom's phone. Would you be able to meet up to return it?" The phone hung up, and when we called it back, it said the number you have reached is no longer in service. A month went by, and we found the phone in the passenger side door of my mom's car that was always locked.

Another cell phone experience is that my mom and dad had an older cell phone, and it would be off and dead in a drawer. The phone would ring in the middle of the night. My dad would get so freaked out by this. He told us that he removed the battery from the phone and left it in his drawer. Then he put the phone in our attached garage. He would get woken up to the phone still ringing in the garage with no battery in it.

When he was working for a company, my dad was in control of the company, group lottery tickets. He always kept the tickets in his top sock drawer of the dresser, tied with an elastic band. Every time the lottery went, he would check them to see if they had won. Well, it was time for him to check the tickets one day, and they weren't in his sock drawer. My parents flipped the house upside down, trying to find these tickets. He was so stressed out because it was time to go and check them, and he didn't know what people were going to think. It was a couple weeks later now, and people were accusing him of taking the winnings. He was stressed to the max. One morning my dad yelled out to my mom to come into their bedroom, and guess what? There the tickets were, at the top drawer of his dresser, placed right on the top of his socks.

The creepy moments continued

This was most definitely one of the times that is like a scary movie moment for me. I was getting ready for highschool one morning, and I was doing my hair and makeup in the bathroom. I kid you not, I heard someone yell out, help me, and I was the *only* one in the bathroom. I ran out of the bathroom so fast after that. I yelled to my mom and explained what happened, and she told me I was crazy and to go to school. This was probably wrong of me to say, but I told her because she didn't believe me that the ghosts were going to haunt her that day. I had gone to school and completely forgot all about what had happened during that morning. When I arrived home from school, she was curled up on the couch crying and said, "How dare you say the ghosts were going to haunt me." I'll also add she owned an at-home daycare at the time, and I am aware now that children can sometimes see spirits more often than adults can. She went on telling me what happened. She said that the one daycare kid came to her and asked, "Why are you not feeding that little girl?" My mom very quickly replied, "What little girl?" The child pointed to somewhere where there was no child physically to be seen by her. She went on to share that later that day, the little girl called my mom into the playroom and said, "Why are you not listening to that little girl crying for help?" Let's just say my mom had to tell the parents about this because she didn't want the parents to think my mom wasn't caring for one of the children that wasn't physically there.

The medium would soon be called

This last story was the last call for our family dealing with these spirits. It was a Tuesday morning, and I remember that because I was off from my spa job and my sister was home. We were so excited to have a girls' day and go downtown Toronto shopping. When we were getting ready, we both heard a massive bang in the basement. Now, my first reaction was that my dad could have had 2 x 4's stacked up along the wall, and they may have fallen on his brand new hardwood floor. I asked my sister if she would come downstairs with me to check? She quickly replied with no way. I was so worried my dad would be so mad if his floor was damaged. So I called my boyfriend, and told him there was a super loud bang downstairs and I asked if he could stay on the phone while I went to check it out. He agreed. When I went downstairs, not a thing was out of place. So I went back upstairs and told my sister and called my dad. My dad said he was busy and for me to go back down and check again, but he had to go. So I called my boyfriend back and went downstairs again. When I went downstairs this time though, I noticed that the bathroom door was shut that wasn't shut a moment ago. My heart dropped; I went to the door like a crazy person, and if it was a movie, I would guess that everyone watching would be saying, "Don't open the door." But I did, and I kid you not friend, I felt a feeling on my right arm. The same as if you were to feel a brush of someone walking past you. Holy jeepers, I felt that on my right arm. For those of you who don't know what happens when hardwood is first put down, for the first little bit when people walk on it, a creaking sound is normal. I share this because right after I felt the feeling on my right arm, the floor creaked right in front of me. Immediately after, my boyfriend asked, "What was that noise?" I replied in a terrified tone, "What noise?" He said, "Just a second ago, there was a weird sound." I told him as I ran up the stairs quickly, "I just felt something on my arm and the floor creaked in front of me." I told him I was going to go and call my dad. As soon as my dad picked up, I burst into tears because I was terrified. I told him what had happened, and he said, "Nicole, you and your sister, get out of that house and don't go back in until someone is there with you." My sister and I left petrified to go shopping as a distraction. When we arrived back home, my mom had called the medium to set up a time to arrive and give us some guidance.

The truth is found almost a decade later

When the medium arrived, she knew nothing but our first names. It was a very weird greeting as she had brought her pet parrot along with her boyfriend. She came inside, and immediately went to my sister's room on the main floor. She said the spirits had shown her they liked this room, and she believed the spirits were there for my sister. When my sister heard that, she was completely freaked out, to say the least. The medium then walked into the basement, and she immediately said the spirits were extremely strong down here, and she looked right at me. At this point, it was my mom and me downstairs with her as my dad and sister were freaked out by the entire process. She then cleared her throat and asked me, "Did you used to have your room upstairs?" I replied quickly, "Yes, the room you entered where you said the spirits were here for my sister was my old room before I moved down into the basement." She laughed a little and said, "That all makes a little more sense now, I'm sorry for the confusion when I was upstairs I felt like the spirits were drawn to your sister, but now that I'm here in the basement, I realize the spirits are actually here for you." I slowly replied while hesitating about what she was going to answer back, "Okay, well, what do they want with me?" I kid you not, I was petrified to hear her response. She said, "They are actually here to protect you. You have heard a little girl and felt things before, haven't you?" I couldn't hold back the tears, I was feeling so many emotions at once. I was terrified, yet I wondered why they were there for me, so through the tears, I replied with a yes.

She told us how there were three spirits present in the home, and they were from the 50s. There was a little girl with reddish hair with a man who was related to her who couldn't protect her from her death. The man that attacked her was also present. She continued by saying that the family member was off in the distance and the other man looked like a dark shadow, wearing a top hat and a long trench coat. This was interesting because my sister explained that exact little girl previously, and well, you know the other interactions after reading this so far.

Guardian angel

She followed with very reassuring words. She said, "These spirits have actually followed you from another house, and they are harmless, but they like to make themselves known. They will move things or do things to show you all that they are here." I asked her, "What does this all have to do with why they're here for me?" She said, "I remember saying the last time you called to remove these spirits that the spirits weren't done doing what they needed to do here." She paused for a minute and asked me, "Were you in a car accident?" I looked at my mom in shock because I had no idea how this woman could have known this and I told her yes. She said, "Nicole, you could feel like someone was there with you protecting you through that, correct?" I replied, "When I was flipping, as you can feel the pressure of something underneath you as you sit down, that is what I felt along with my head felt like it was being held in place." She said, "But you don't share that with many people, right?" I explained to her that I didn't share a lot about that time in my life because I couldn't understand how I… And before I could get the rest of it out, she finished my sentence, about how you made it out alive because you shouldn't have as it was a serious accident. She then asked, "Was there a circle over your head in the car that you found?" I said, "When my mom and I looked at the car afterwards I noticed a perfect circle shape around my head." She said the little girl wants you to know she was the one who saved you that day. I immediately cried so hard because I had always wondered about that day, and now I was told that this little girl is like a guardian angel of mine. The medium asked me, "Are you crying because you're scared or because you're sad." I told her, "I get scared because sometimes I feel pressure at the end of my bed like someone is watching me but also sad because I couldn't help her like she did for me." She said, "Nicole, the little girl wants you to know, she is sorry she scared you, and she just wants to make sure you're safe." I asked her, "What is the explanation about me hearing her asking for help?" She said, "This little girl was about eleven when she was murdered by the man in the black coat, with a gun and a knife and her family member that is here with her in the spirit world couldn't protect her from this, and he wants to make sure she passes over to the light and isn't bothered anymore." She looked at me and said, "Nicole, she makes me feel like you're not telling or saying something." I looked at my mom and put my hands right up to my face, and cried. My mom said, "It's okay, Nicole" as she rubbed my back and said, "You can tell her." I told the medium, "I was actually attacked at the age of eleven by a guy with a knife and a gun; he told me he was going to let my mom watch him kill me that day." She said, "That day, you noticed that he just let go both his hands almost as if someone was stopping him, and the little girl wants you to know that she was doing her best to protect you that day." I cried again because I said I couldn't be more grateful for the things that she's protected me from, but I'm sorry that no one could have done that for her. She finished off by asking if there were any other questions. I said, "Is it okay if we pass all the spirits on to the light?" She said, "I believe it's time; they have done what they have come here to do." So she said a saying, burnt some sage, and gave us Latin sayings to put on our wall décor around the house in places where no one else could see, but if these spirits or others attempted to come here, that they would be confused and not stay. She explained that with us living with spirits our whole life, we were accepting of them, but they were actually there as our families guarding angels. She did share that if something happened in our lives where we would need some protection that our family had lots of spirit guides around to do their part.

This was very comforting to hear because no matter what was to come, I had felt that our family truly did have this protection from another source as guardian angels looking out for each of us. Even if that meant that these ones were okay to move into the light. As she did that, my heart felt an odd sense of warmth for this little girl that I had never met and felt a little bit of her pain for in that moment I knew her truth. She did her all to keep me alive. How does one sit with that information?

Anxiety appeared

To tell you the truth, I couldn't sleep in my room in the basement for a year and a half without having an insane amount of pressure on my chest like I was having an anxiety attack. I didn't know that then, but I know that now. So I either took a shot of Nyquil every night and slept downstairs, or the living room couch was the place I could find comfort being not too far from the rest of my family on the main floor. Even though I found comfort in knowing why this little girl was around me in the spirit world, it sometimes wasn't enough when I would remember some of the terrifying things my family had experienced.

The spirit guides returned

The medium was also right when she told us that the spirits would come back when I needed them.

In 2014, I had just been picked up by my boyfriend from work as I had chest pains. The moment I got in our truck, I couldn't take it anymore. I had felt such intense pressure in my chest, and I explained it was like I wanted to run but I couldn't, or I had just drank a bunch of energy drinks, and my heart was pounding. We rushed to the emergency. I thought I was having a heart attack, and when my boyfriend moved his foot from the brake pedal to the gas, I was immediately hunched over in the front seat sobbing in pain. The emergency staff rushed me to a room where I was met with a nurse right away. I had test after test. They came back with my ECG showing an abnormal test, and I was to wait for an appointment with the cardiologist.

It felt like forever, but during the time that I had to wait, I was prescribed steroids and inflammatory medication. While taking them, I had little to no pain, but I had about twenty-five out of thirty plus side effects. I was working at the doctor's office at the time, so I called the doctor I worked for, and he said I needed to stop the medication immediately. I stopped it all cold turkey, but what I found after that was my body went through withdrawal (so I was told at the time). Every muscle clenched at the same time, and I found no comfort except when I was in a hot bath.

I was finally seen by the cardiologist, and they did an ECG, Echo, (heart ultrasound) stress test, and a heart monitor. The ECG showed normal at this time, the echo showed inflammation and fluid around the sack surrounding my heart. During my stress test, I couldn't be pushed very far without having pain and feeling like I was going to pass out. The cardiologist gave me a heart monitor to go home with. We actually went to the mountains that weekend, and I wasn't aware that the altitude change was going to make my chest pains worse. So when I had to log in when I had pains, I also noted that I was in the mountains.

I was finally seen by my family doctor to follow up with the cardiologist's report, and my doctor said, "Nicole, I am sorry to say, but you have pericarditis." I had no idea what pericarditis was and she went on to explain exactly what they found in the echo, which was inflammation and fluid around the sack of my heart.

This was a long road ahead of healing, but while I was healing, I could feel the presence of the spirits around me become stronger and stronger. Anytime I went to the basement to go to the laundry room or the shower, I would immediately feel like someone was watching me. I was worried at first when I started to feel these things happen, and then I remembered that I had guardian angels looking out for me. But it didn't make it less scary at times when they were trying to make themselves known.

One morning I was standing at the kitchen sink, and everyone else was sleeping except my sister's boyfriend. I could hear him in the living room playing video games, but all of a sudden I saw a shadow by the hallway. The ceiling in this kitchen was a drop ceiling that had plastic light covers. While I was standing at the sink, I saw something out of my right eye, and when I looked, the plastic piece was lifting up and fell right out of the ceiling. I knew at that exact moment it was the spirits making it very clear that they were there.

When my healing came to an end, and I was back to perfect health, I no longer felt the presence of spirits in the home.

Life is sometimes so interesting even with situations like this when there are moments of complete terror but also so much comfort to me on a spiritual level. To know that those spirits, whether they were the same from when I was a child or different, I had an entire other level of protection surrounding me at all times in my life, and they would make themselves present whenever I needed them most. Like I said, this chapter wasn't to convince anyone to believe in the spirit world, life after death, or ghosts, whichever word you want to call this topic. But to show how interesting life is sometimes, the greater plan with these situations have come full circle. I found answers that I never knew I would find. Along with being reminded of how much protection I have along with my family members. I will forever find comfort knowing this is so.

12

SPLASH PAD ONE WYATT ZERO

I can't protect him from everything

June 27th, 2021, Andrew, my mom, Wyatt, and I were enjoying an amazing moment together, soaking in our first time at the outdoor splash pad. The water was everywhere, and we were all having so much fun until the last five minutes of our time there. Wyatt was running around having the time of his life. He ran through the water that was spraying up out of the ground. His little face was covered in water, and he couldn't see and tripped. Now take a moment to realize this was in a matter of seconds.

Of course, the initial response from him was tears. I picked him up and comforted him, reminding him that he was going to be okay and I was there for him, and I was sorry that had happened to him. The ground at that splash pad was really rough with a bumpy texture. He had two scrapes on his knees. To some, it may be a scrape on a child's knee, but to this momma bear it was something that couldn't be immediately fixed. No matter how hard I looked at it. I couldn't turn back time. I had to accept and trust in the healing process. A process I trusted, yes, this sounds silly, I know. But to my little love, that was just having fun and now crying, holding me so tightly, whispering, ouch momma, ouch. I wanted to go back in time and wrap him in bubble wrap, but that's not life. I said to my husband on the drive home as I was watching my little man champ it out in the rearview mirror, "You know babe, we cannot protect him from the world, but how we respond when he needs us is the important lesson learned on this day." He replied, "That's all we can do."

Trust the healing process

So I had a moment of panic. What do I do to fix this? Can I use adult polysporin on a two-year-old? Can I put hydrogen peroxide on him? What bandages are best to use for this? Why are there a million and one bandage options? The anxious momma bear spiral was happening. So I took a deep breath, and I trusted the pharmacist. Kids polysporin and fancy clear bandages.

All was good until I needed to change the bandages. It was like duct tape on someone's skin. I immediately said out loud to my husband, "What have I done?" He cried, but again he was a champ about it.

The body's natural job is to protect ourselves no matter how small we are. It was amazing to witness how he changed his routine to adapt to this healing process. He would sit and play with his cars with his feet on the ground in a squatting position; he would get up on the couch and bed feet first and stand up instead. Such a small human with mind-blowing resilience.

The bigger lesson

Sometimes as a parent, I think I have so much to teach this little love when really, some days, I learn more from him and am reminded of life's basic knowledge.

- Trust in the process.
- You can't rush the healing process.
- Try to live your life while learning to change your routine to adapt if needed.
- There are multiple ways to do the same thing.

That's the beauty and truth of motherhood, though. There has to be a big enough emotional connection for a moment in time to make a lasting impact on your life and stay a memory. This moment along with many more to still come, is what makes me believe that life has a greater plan.

Who knew the last five minutes at a kids' splash pad and five seconds of time could teach this momma bear so much.

13

MANIFEST AND HOLD THE FAITH

Through my own personal healing, I have found the power within during harder and difficult situations. I know from my delivery with Wyatt that the mind only knows what you feed it. When we, as a family, were told that Wyatt would need intensive dental surgery, this was a moment in my family's life we *never* saw coming.

When situations come up that we may never have expected, we get to choose how we act, either react or respond. I chose to take a deep breath and respond. I knew I would manifest the night before and the day of my son's surgery, by continuing to focus on what I wanted to happen, all while keeping the energy calm and protected. Reminding myself that I needed to be brave every step of the way.

Be in the present moment

The night before Wyatt's surgery, we created a space that was calm along with us all being present in the evening. We were enjoying and soaking in each other's time. We, as a family, reminded ourselves why we were doing this. It was for Wyatt's future health, and we were choosing to better his future from that moment on.

As a family, we continued to remind ourselves with the affirmations that we're brave, strong, kind, courageous, could do anything, and then we'd say our names.

We took a moment to explain to Wyatt what was going to happen and prepared him for the night ahead and the next day.

We shared that he wasn't able to have food or be able to nurse past a certain time for his safety. He so calmly agreed, and he said he understood. I also told him that I would be sleeping downstairs, and he would be safe sleeping beside dada. We prepared and kept our nighttime routine as normal as possible. Except we let Wyatt sleep with an outfit on so that it was an easy transition right to the car in the morning.

We understood as a family that it was Wyatt's first time ever without me in the evening and understood that he usually needed me for comfort to sleep. We were going into this evening with so much calmness and understanding for everyone. The evening was a breeze with an incredible sense of calm.

Wyatt nursed just before the time he was allowed, and he slept so well for Andrew. When he did wake up, he snuggled into Andrew's arm, Andrew soothed him right back to sleep in a calm, natural manner, and they both loved this time in the night together. I slept so well knowing that Andrew had my back along with Wyatt's. Andrew has an inner calmness about him and is a kick-ass dad with so many strengths.

The morning I woke, and I heard Wyatt wake up. He was crying for me; I went to him and explained that I knew he was tired and that I would prepare him to go into the vehicle, and he could fall right back to sleep with a cozy warm blanket. He ended up falling asleep soundly in the car before we could make ten minutes down the road. I woke him up just enough to walk into the hospital, where I reminded myself of the reasons for doing it. 'It's for his safety. These people are professionals. We are strong. We can do this.'

We do this with positivity and affirmations

We would wait for the next steps from the staff and go into the OR with an at ease and calm energy. I kept reminding myself while we waited that I wanted Wyatt to see my brave face during that time. I kept saying, "Today will try to shake me but I will not let that win because I am stronger than I know." I kept repeating over and over positive words to Wyatt. That I was going to be right there the whole time with him and that the dentist was going to just take a look at his teeth and put some shiny things on them.

When the moment came for the anesthesiologist to have a chat with me, he explained what would happen and what was normal. He said, "Usually, my parents have to hold the kiddos down." I replied, "I won't have to do that with Wyatt, as he's such a calm child."

Our name was called, 'oh goodness me,' it was my turn to bring Wyatt to prep for surgery. I let the medical staff know that I would need a minute to do our ritual just before he was going to be put out. Wyatt and I got a brief moment while he was having the anesthesiologist place the gas over his face;

the professional couldn't believe I didn't have to pin Wyatt down, and he didn't even have to add any pressure to keep him still. I held my emotions back so well, knowing that he needed to see my strength and bravery. I got these words out with ease.

We both looked at each other and while he was getting sleepy I said out loud.

'I am brave.

I am kind.

I am strong.

I am courageous.

I can do anything.

My name is Wyatt.'

The nurse standing behind me touched my back and said, "You are one brave momma."

The lady told me I could follow her out. She said to me, "Don't worry, we've got your son." I said in the kindest way possible through the tears, "You better take care of my son." I find the courage and strength to leave Wyatt with the people who know best for this moment. I trust and have faith, and I hold the space for the universe, along with our angel's watching above and spirits around us to do their work and protect him and be with him when we cannot.

When I walked out, I could hardly breathe with sheer emotion along with the silly mask on my face. I wanted so badly to get out to see my husband and my mom. I walked up to where they were parked. My mom asked how I was, and I said to her I just had to walk. For me, sometimes standing still isn't even possible. My mom and husband asked if I want them to come. I couldn't even respond. My husband came out of the truck and gave me the biggest hug. I told him I had to walk and just breathe. Us as a family, we feel the feelings, talk and let the feelings pass.

I took this time with my husband to tell him everything that happened as he wasn't allowed to come inside. We made a video to show Wyatt one day, and we chose to remind each other that we were so epically strong, including our little champ himself. We sat with the time during his surgery and reminded ourselves and held the space for having faith.

I took massive deep breaths called my sister and my dad. We went back to the vehicle, and my mom met me at the back with a bag filled with chocolates. I sat in the back eating almost an entire bag of mini Reese's.

My phone rang; it had only been about twenty or thirty minutes. The person said Wyatt would be waking up soon, so they would like to bring me to the recovery room so when he woke, I would be there with him.

Reunited and comfort

I heard Wyatt crying. The nurse came out with Wyatt in her arms. As she was walking, he was trying to flail out of her arms. She passed him to me, and he was doing everything in his power to get comfy and understand where he was. His body was so limp, and he wasn't able to hold his head up. I was doing my best to stay calm. I was whispering in his ear, "It's momma baby, I'm here, you did it, Wyatt. "I told him he was safe and I held his hand so tight. I reminded him again of our positive words; he was brave. He was strong. He was kind. He was courageous. He could do anything. He was going to change the world. His name was Wyatt. Wyatt took this so well he snuggled right into my arms and nursed. I asked him if he was proud of himself, and through all the drowsiness, he quickly answered, "Yes, momma."

The nurse came back to check on his levels, she said. "Wyatt's oxygen levels are low; it would be best if you try to move him around to get things flowing." So I woke him up and asked if he wanted some juice and a popsicle. He agreed, and the nurse came back; she rechecked all his vitals, and said everything was okay.

We reviewed everything with the surgeons, and they said everything went as planned, and they were so proud of Wyatt as he did a great job.

We conquered this

We went out to the car, and Andrew gave him the biggest hug and told him that he was so proud of him and asked Wyatt if he was proud of himself. They had an incredible moment together. My mom gave him a hug and told him that she was so proud of him too. She showed him this bright yellow smiley face balloon to celebrate. He was a little bit tired and just wanted to go to sleep in the car.

We arrived back home with a huge surprise for him and relaxed for the next couple of days. Wyatt recovered with ease and was back to his perfect self in no time.

Visualize and hold the faith until

I wrote how the day was going to look eight days before his surgery. Then I added the specific details after writing this chapter. I visualized and held space for how I would manifest this time in our lives. I signed the bottom. Love, your younger self.

Of course, I added all the exact daily details but not much changed from how I visualized it, and there is so much power in sharing this with you because someone once shared this with me, and it served me so well during this time. I could have chosen to be so fearful, allowing anxiety and panic to sink in. But how would that have served my family and me?

So during any time in your life where you can choose fear, worry, anxiety, or panic, I hope you choose to breathe, visualize everything you want to happen, hold the faith and continue holding the faith until it shows up the way you want. Thinking of nothing else but what you want. I promise you this, your future self will be so proud of your younger self for doing just that.

14

OVERLOADED AND BURNT OUT

"Nicole, you have emotional overload," said my counselor.

As a very emotional person, I knew what the beginning part of that meant but not the overloaded. I could handle so much I couldn't be overloaded. *WRONG!*

Trying to do everything is taking a toll

I was so used to doing, doing, doing, and being there for everyone, except for one person, *Me*. Going through motherhood is rewarding but also moments of guilt always flooded me. Guilt of self-care, 'how dare I choose to care for myself versus spending quality time with my husband that I missed dearly and leave my son so I could go for a walk or bath alone. I already spend so much of my time alone with no adults all day. Why would I want to go and do more stuff alone? That just sounds ridiculous.'

Until all the excitement and emotions wore off after the summer of 2021. It was a long year and a half without seeing family and friends. The time finally came when I was reunited with family members; this was the moment I would still give any time or anything for.

The time was amazing with every guest; I gave so much of my time to spend with them that I forgot about myself. I should have taken advantage of showering more or gone on a date night with my husband seeing as the last time prior was almost two years ago. But again, guilt crept in. How could I leave to go and shower, go for a walk, go for dinner without them? I wanted to soak up as much time with each of them as I could.

I will also share that I am a very empathic person, so I literally feel everything everyone feels. I think of myself feeling everything and walking through what others are going through. When everyone arrived, left, and everything in between. I felt it all, and it ripped my heart out when they each had to leave, never mind the never-ending wonders and questions my two-year-old had. He had no understanding of distance, and I couldn't stop thinking how bad I wanted them to come back and do one more thing together. Never mind how my son felt.

Plus, on top of all that, add my son's unexpected dental surgery right in the middle. This was the weight of the world. I was holding all my emotions in to be strong for my little person so he could also be strong. Being strong for so many people and pushing my own care aside was taking its toll on me.

So long story short, I was told I had an emotional overload, couldn't keep my mind on one thing, I was overwhelmed, crying all the time, couldn't get one task completed without trying to complete everything else, was never relaxing, and always going.

Forced to care for myself

So I took the following week and was mindful of taking time for myself, fully grounding in nature, and forgetting the to-do list. Only for the end of the week coming to an end, and then feeling like I had to play catch up. The result of this was physical symptoms showing up, and the next night the dizziness arrived.

It subsided a little as we spent the weekend outdoors to ground ourselves in nature camping as a family. It was time to leave and go home. We had to go home the same way we came. The only difference was my husband was the one in the driver's seat. We were driving home on a dirt road; I was no longer the one in the driver seat. Meaning someone else was in control of a vehicle on a dirt road. When we first approached the road, nothing even came to mind; it was when I realized the window wasn't down out of habit. Then I heard the rocks hitting the car and the trailer. I had a PTSD experience and a panic attack. I controlled it pretty well and suppressed the feelings.

Nothing good comes from suppressed feelings

Guess what? Everything came back full throttle Sunday, and by Tuesday, I couldn't stop the dizziness and was disoriented as the room kept spinning. I got up in the middle of the night to go pee, and it was really bad. I almost fell into the toilet, and when I stood back up, I could only feel better if I was holding onto something, and it took me about two minutes before I could walk.

On Tuesday, the chest pains, dizziness, and spins only got stronger. I decided to go to the doctor, and when I was driving to the clinic while using my left hand, I had pressure under my left armpit and chest pains on the left side of my upper chest. The doctor told me I had Benign positional vertigo after doing a couple different movements and watching my eyes, and I was told to rest but first go to get blood work and an ECG right away. I was also told by the doctor if I had any form of headache or pressure after our appointment to go to urgent care. She gave me a prescription for seasickness, and I took one of those. Off I went to go get my bloodwork and ECG.

As per the doctor's orders, I went home to rest for two hours only to be woken up with a massive headache. Ice pick feeling on the top right part of my head and pressure behind my left eye. So there I was on the way to the urgent care. They did an ECG, bloodwork, and a bunch of exercises to see how I was functioning. I'd already done all that earlier in the day but they didn't have the test results back, so they did it all again.

What happens mentally shows up physically

The doctor had the results, "Nicole, you have Costochondritis which is inflammation of the chest wall on the left side." The other test results came back with nothing concerning so she went on to add that benign positional vertigo could last for six days to as long as eight weeks.

I knew immediately I brought it all on myself. I was dealing with emotional overload for the last two weeks, and on top of that, I had a PTSD experience and had an anxiety and panic attack. Why I share this is because I researched the type of vertigo I had, and it said when the body experiences high stress, anxiety, or PTSD, it can cause the inner ear to be thrown off and cause that type of vertigo.

New perspective

So this shifted my perspective, just like the airplane demonstration. You cannot save someone else unless you put your own oxygen mask on.

I was making sure everyone else was okay and cared for but was emptying my own tank. I was frustrated with myself as I had spent the last year learning that what you focus on continues to grow, and what you think about in the mind all shows up in the physical body.

This was my brick wall. I was my own bolder in my path.

What I also know is, I am the one who is learning and walking through this unfamiliar territory and I realize perfection isn't welcome here; I don't have to do it all, I can ask for help, I can step away because it gives room for others to connect, grow and learn without me. The beauty is that when I am filling up my own cup, I can pour more into others.

So the next few days, I was so present; I was transparent and vulnerable. I thought, how could I not have been aware that I was doing this to myself? But I realized I couldn't be alone. And guess what? I was not alone, many people have experienced this, and it's okay. So I learned the lesson being taught. Listen to the body and repair it.

I wrapped myself in white ribbon, meditated, focused on healing through hypnotherapy, acupuncture sessions, and transformed my thoughts on self-care. Self-care isn't optional; it is mandatory. Because it is only when we love ourselves and fill our own cups that we can truly love others and pour into them from our best, strongest self.

Love yourself today and every day!

15

MY LOWEST OF ALL LOWS

As I sit here in all the overwhelm, I can't seem to identify who I even am. I look in the mirror, and I don't even recognize the woman staring back at me. I have no idea when this loss of who I am occurred. I just want to find that sparkle within. I want to stop smiling through the fake smile. I want to yell from the rooftops that I can't keep doing everything alone. I want to know that when I ask for help, the help is there. I want to be able to know how to express myself while not worrying about how it will affect someone else. By doing this, I am blowing out my own light within. By me trying to care more about other people's feelings over my own, I am the one blowing out my own light within. I had to write that twice because it is only in writing this down that I am understanding how much damage I am doing to myself.

I wonder how long it will take for me to listen to the words I say to others. How long will it take for me to be able to go an entire day without feeling like I haven't done enough? How long will it be till I feel like I have accomplished what I could do rather than all the things I never got to? How long will it take me to reach my goals without having to be so hard on myself? If I step away from my life or, god forbid, the house doesn't look like no one lives inside, maybe I won't feel the weight of the world without guilt to do something for me.

I hope one day I can sit by myself and hear my breath and my heartbeat and be still and calm instead of being frustrated that I "should" be doing something else.

I know the day will come when I recognize this woman staring back. The day when I will look in the mirror and be so proud of what this woman has gone through. But as of now, I see a woman who hates the reflection staring back. I hate her because I wish she would get over herself and not let the shit she's been through trip her up time and time again. The person staring back at me, I know she's been through a lot. Some days I have so much patience for her, and others, I am so ready to throw the towel in and call it quits. Life would be easier if I just quit.

I never came this far to only come this far

But then, that stubborn woman who will *never give up* is the strongest voice inside. I did not make it this far to only come this far. I did not overcome things that most humans wouldn't be able to find a positive side to give up because I don't know who I am. I am stronger than that. I know I am capable and willing. Well, most days, I do. Today isn't one of those days. Today I am lost in the darkness. Today I have no idea who I am.

I know I won't always feel like this. I know I won't look at my body in complete disgust. I know I will be able to feel okay. As for now, I will just take one step at a time. Breathe. Keep going. I will choose to go on despite how I am feeling now. I have an amazing life. I know I will be reunited with the person that is in there. The one that has the fire lit within like a dragon. I just am not sure how long I want to wait for that woman to arrive. Holding the pieces together until she is found has a weight like no other. But eventually, the weight has to give. Eventually, this extra weight will be lifted off me. As for now, I feel like I'm standing on the edge of the deep end in a pool, and just as you want to swim back to the shallow part to stand and not feel the pressure of the water at your neck. Something is keeping me staying there. Standing with the pressure of the water at my neck. I can't wait for the day to release that pressure. My own individual pressures that I have put on myself. I know all that personal work I have done for myself. All the hours at counseling sessions I know will be worth it when I start to feel like me again.

Hope

And I will owe it all to hope. The hope I had during my darkest days. Remembering even the stars can't shine without darkness. So through the darkness, I will continue to shine. Even on the days when I don't want to. Even on the days when I want to throw the towel in and, most importantly, on the days where I want to quit. Because no one likes a quitter, and I'm most definitely not going to quit on me. Having hope for all the moments, I will later experience will be so worth it for pushing through. One thing I never realized was I was never really alone. As I always had me.

The feeling when being reunited with family or an old childhood friend. I cannot wait to feel the joy overflow within me when I meet the part of me that loves me. The part of me that is so happy I live the life I do. The part of me that uses my voice all the time. The part of me that loves me. I will hold that visual for now and be excited for that day.

For that day, I will be whole. I will no longer be lost. The me I was meant to be will be found. I will be me and look in the mirror with tears rolling down my cheeks, thinking to myself, damn girl, you finally arrived.

16

HEALING THROUGH THE STORM

One of the things I was taught by one of my counselors throughout my years of personal development and healing, is. If you want to know what you want or need to work on personally, ask yourself this question. If you were to teach or raise a child, what would be something you would teach them? Second, what would be something you would do differently from your childhood?

By answering the above questions, you will find the deep-rooted things you need to heal, repair, reprogram and work through to make you grow into your highest divine self.

I truly believe the path that led me to the journey of motherhood and raising my son Wyatt led me to my self-discovery, my desire and need for personal growth, and has become my guide to healing myself through this journey called life. By doing this, I have found that every part of my story was and is still part of the greater plan. Nothing can be rushed, and everything shows up at the time that we need it most. I believe this also goes for healing.

What I would like to do for the remainder of our time together is to create a space for you to sit with yourself. I would like to ask you some questions, whether you decide to do anything with them is a personal decision. Yes, I understand I cannot make you do anything, but what I hope is that I inspired you, maybe even for one minute. I hope that you, yes, *you*, the individual that took the time to read this book and make it this far. I hope you take the time to dive into personal growth, and if it's uncomfortable, I hope you lean in. I hope you do your best to pivot and see from a new perspective and sit with your own magnifying glass at times in your life. To discover for yourself the greater plan that life had and still has for you.

Dig deep

Have you ever asked yourself any of these questions?

1. When am I going to wake up and no longer be bothered by this?
2. I wish I didn't have things happen to me because why do they have to get to me all these years later?
3. I just want to know when I'm going to be okay?
4. How do I go on from here, and how do I not let these situations control my life?
5. What do I do from this point on because I don't want to be like this anymore?

I want you to take a moment to reflect. Have you ever asked yourself these questions or something similar?

If you have, please know that this is your moment of growth. You are listening to that intuitive voice within you that you no longer want to accept the experience prior to this to "control" the way you show up in the world. I would love to honor this space and just tell you that I am proud of you. And now ask yourself, are you proud of yourself? Asking yourself questions like this takes a level of awareness to realize and to decide that you want to change and grow. That being said, I, of course, had all of the above questions and more when it came to my early twenties when I moved to Alberta. I never realized before because I've always been around the closest people that I love, but when you give yourself some time to step away from everything you've known and start fresh. I found that I had a lot of personal growth to do.

I experienced meeting new people and having very little trust. I experienced working in a new environment and when I had male clients, I would immediately feel trapped when I shut the door to my treatment room. I had to walk home alone in the dark during the early mornings and evenings, and I would never relax. I would constantly look over my shoulder and hold something between my fingers. I would come up against making a decision in my life, and I would look for others to guide me. I would keep quiet with my opinions when I would be screaming inside. I wasn't able to express myself when I was so frustrated or angry without crying or finding the words. I remember taking the city bus when I didn't have a car, and every time I stepped on the bus, I wanted to puke when I thought of some of the things I saw when I was a younger child. I never felt safe in my own world. My mind was cautious, worried, stressed, and always going. Sometimes I had learned that this was helpful in my life but I was finding out that by living my life in that state it wasn't going to be an enjoyable life. So I sat with myself, which I'll share that I hated being alone. I hated the feeling, I hated the thoughts that would come into my mind, and I hated talking about the way I was feeling with people because no one ever knew the entire story. I had an insane amount of shame for my story; I felt it was something to hide, I *never* wanted people to know and that I would die with these stories. These were my thoughts in 2014 and what I found happening was the light within was dying slowly as the days went on. When I was suppressing and not facing what I needed to, it was making me feel this warmth and glow when I "needed" to be and when I was alone, I was fading into the parts of me that were pulling me down. Let me be clear, I am far from perfect and yes some days those previous thoughts still try to sneak in but I remind myself what is done, is done. I am safe and I have received all the things I have dreamed of. So with that being said, now my current twenty-one year healing journey self would do this, I would thank my attacker. Crazy to see that shift right. I know I cannot believe I just came to that realization. But I would thank him because this was the tragedy that led me home. Just like a connect the dot image, the image wouldn't be complete if a dot was missing. So what would I thank him for, you may be thinking? I would thank him for the strength and courage that I found through healing. The awareness of bullying. The awareness of support. The awareness of living. Awareness has been and will continue to be the greatest agent for my healing and for change.

So again, the awareness to recognize this is the first step. Through doing this I release the power the situation held on me and I take all my power back! I am me, a powerful being that is in full control.

The second step for me was to quiet the opinions in my head that I had about counseling. I thought anyone who needed counseling was weak. How could I take up the time of someone who may need it for more of a life or death reason? Even to this day, if I'm up against a difficult situation, sometimes my mind will go toward old habits and beliefs. This is a lifelong journey through healing. But it's learning some tips and things that really help when these moments come up. So I'll continue to share what I've learned that helps me, and while doing this, maybe it will be helpful one day if you ever need it.

I believe that if you are the most knowledgeable person in your network, you need to expand your network. So I went searching for people who were on similar self-healing, personal growth, and wanting to become their best selves journeys.

What I found were healers and counselors I could lean on. I learned about the power of meditation, which has now become part of my daily practice. I learned about having a hypnotherapy counselor. I learned about the shadow work method. I leaned into personal growth, I took courses, and found mentors that I could trust. I learned the importance of living from the end result. I was a student at this time in my life. I believe this statement that I was told by one of my mentors has so much truth. *When the student is ready, the teacher will arrive.*

Lessons learned through healing

Through these teaching moments, I've learned these things. In order to have success with dealing with PTSD, it is all dependable on your support systems and the power within you to become your best self. Our brain's key focus is to keep us safe during some situations that are all created from our minds. Yes, this may sound like a mental battle. I know because through the process of digging deep, I had many days that were exactly that, a mental battle. But your brain holds onto signs to keep and continues to make sure you're safe.

Overthinking has been something I have dealt with for a long time. I've even shared this in earlier chapters, but what I found by overthinking this actually leads to downward spirals. Which is not a good place to be for growth and positivity.

Along with self-doubt. Self-doubt is the greatest dream stealer out there because most people don't even start what they desire. They are too afraid to start and make a move forward. Allowing self-doubt to be present doesn't send anyone down a positive path.

The key to healing is to be patient because sometimes anxiety likes to hold onto any slight bit of uncertainty. Learning what to do to find safety and calm during life and before anxiety sets in takes so much inner strength.

Tools and tips for healing

I truly believe, and I have also been taught, that the only way to show up, think different thoughts, and to be different is to reprogram the brain. This is where affirmations are key. An example of some that I always say are, I am doing my best at healing myself along the way. I know life has a greater plan for me, and I will keep going. I choose to walk over things that used to trip me up.

When you have any moments or feelings that you do not want, as fast as you can snap your fingers, train your mind to pivot. Healing is a process; it takes time, and before you know it, these questions will become second nature in the moment.

Ask yourself these things:

1. What are my feelings that are uncomfortable?
2. What are my clues and triggers?
3. What is happening that I am convincing myself to be true?
4. What uncertainty is presenting that I am convinced is true?
5. What would my younger self need to be told?
6. What message can I remind myself of going forward?
7. What are my re-parenting lessons?
8. Transition from reacting to responding to any situation. (This is the one that made such a massive change for me)
9. Be willing to practice all the time.
10. Always remember to be kind and love yourself where you are at today.

Remember, we can only take people as far as we have gone ourselves. So be okay with the path you are on because you never know where it may lead you. Continue to share your message and help others as we help where we've been hurt, so others don't hurt in vain.

When I was younger, I used to feel that I wanted to trade spaces with someone else, so I didn't have to feel or deal with the emotions or feelings of what I had gone through. But I am so glad life never worked out like that because of the jealousy

I would have knowing what beautiful, liberating life I have today.

I share this all because I know the other side of all this growth. I want to leave this space below for you to do this ritual that helped me many times in the past.

Tasks for you to decide to complete or not

Write a letter in the space below or on a separate paper to your younger self from the person you are today. I want you to think of all the things you can write about that led you through the journey to the human being you are now.

Now I'd like you to do another ritual with me. You can do this below or find a piece of paper.

First write all the things that are not serving you; these can be old beliefs, how you see yourself or the way you think about something particular to you.

Now I would like you to rewrite the above statements and write something positive. Maybe a positive affirmation or something positive about the person you're becoming.

Lastly, I want you to tear out or tear the paper you wrote the negative things on, the old beliefs you no longer want. Tear them up and burn them. Of course, in a safe place and away from anything that can cause harm. Before you do this, breathe out compassion and love for your younger self and breathe in joy and excitement for the person you're becoming.

Go forward knowing you're never too old to learn and lean into and trust yourself. Always remember your story may inspire others someday, and it could even be a road map for them to get through their difficult times. So share your experience doing these above rituals if you feel called to and pass along what you have learned because this is what this beautiful life is all about. Helping, growing, healing, learning, trusting, and living this beautiful life as our best selves and learning the greater plan for each and every one of us.

17

LIFE CAN BE HEAVY, BUT YOU GET TO DECIDE

I want to do a visual experiment with you.

As you read through this chapter feel free to take your time and soak in the moments, to pause and reflect. (No pun intended)

First I want you to visualize standing at a sink with two face cloths. Now turn on your sink to whatever temperature of water you'd like. Envision soaking each face cloth with water, adding weight to the cloth as you're doing this.

The water being absorbed into each cloth can represent our life events or baggage as some people may call it. Whatever word you choose to use is fine but these moments all happened for you, even though some may have tried to weigh you down. As you hold those two clothes that are getting heavy as the water continues to flow, you now have two choices.

You get to choose what you do with both these soaking wet, weighted down face cloths.

These are your choices. I'll also share that there are no right or wrong answers if you feel like you never signed up to be graded today while reading this. You can take a breath. Your answer isn't right or wrong, it just is.

Option one:

You can choose to scrunch the face cloth up, adding no pressure to the cloth at all, and placing it wherever you choose to let it dry out. Keeping all the water left in the cloth. This can represent leaving all our life events or baggage attached to you. This is the easier decision of the two as this cloth will be dry.....*eventually*.

... Right?

Option two:

You can choose to take that cloth and accept that there is lots of water soaked into it. Take a deep breath, have a moment of understanding and learn that there is a way faster way to get this water out. You *just* have to use a little force and squeeze it as hard as you can. Representing doing some personal growth, healing some life events or baggage which may include going deep into life situations that have happened and using that FORCE.

This may sound like a silly exercise, but the goal is for you to sit and have a moment of reflection and decide how you have been getting rid of the water being absorbed into your face cloth or life events that have happened to you.

Are you going to allow it to weigh you down and take a while to release the extra water weight? Or are you going to put a little more work in and squeeze hard for a little while to release that weight holding you down faster?

The final outcome is two dry cloths.

WELL.....

Eventually two dry cloths.

18

MOUNTAIN PEAK ADVENTURE

I've truly realized that some people get placed in life situations that feel like the bottom or in front of a massive mountain peak that feels impossible to conquer. I believe this happens for the individual to be tested to see if they want what they're working towards bad enough. And for those that do, they get to enjoy the most incredible view, and these intense moments of greatness. While they also grow into the person they were always meant to become.

Cascade mountain

I will never forget the day I hiked Cascade mountain in Banff National Park in Alberta, Canada.

Hiking this mountain was and is a mental push, in my opinion. If you ever get the chance to hike this mountain, I would highly recommend that you do, and no matter what people tell you during the journey, you go and rock it to your best ability.

Some will say the view is good from the parking lot.

Some will say the view is great from halfway up.

Some will even say when you're three-quarters of the way up, 'goodness isn't that view just breathtaking'. They may even ponder that they've made it this far; the view can't get much better than three quarters up the mountain.

That is where those people are wrong. Most of the individuals hiking this mountain will give up just before the MOST UNIMAGINABLE VIEW! They will give up because it gets really hard at that last bit. At the tip-top of that mountain, it's super uncomfortable to push yourself to the depths of the unknown. But what you will discover after doing that sometimes is the most BREATHTAKING MOMENTS. You will see your strength defined. You will be so proud of yourself.

So what voice do you feed in your head?

Are you the parking lot view of the mountain?

Halfway up the mountain?

The three-quarters up the mountain?

Or are you right up to the tip-top of the mountain type of person?

When we aren't sure of what to do we may look to others for the answer for our next move. I will tell you something, friend, honestly, if that person isn't working towards what you are working towards or want to go where you want to go in life, you will just get their opinion. Opinions have *zero* knowledge. You have to learn to trust in yourself, listen to that intuitive feeling you have within and despite what anyone else is doing around you. I hope you keep your head down and stay in your own lane. I hope you listen to what feels best to you. I hope you get to push yourself to limits where you learn more about who you are and your greater purpose in this life. Most importantly, even after all of that, I hope you have a humbled heart for what you have gone through. I hope you found some answers to your questions. I hope you've become clear as to why things happened in your life for you the way they did. I hope you never give up. I hope you know your story and life is happening for you, not to you. I hope you get an exciting feeling like a fire is lit inside you for the greater plan that life has in store for you.

When life tries to see how tough you truly are, remember these words.

You are brave.

You are kind.

You are strong.

You are courageous.

You can do anything.

You are YOU!

And if you find it hard to be you one day, choose to be like a buffalo.

AUTHOR BIO

Nicole Recker is so grateful for everything that has led her to the life she lives. She is forever grateful for the opportunity and blessing to be her, a wife and momma. Her role as a momma has led her to dig deep into personal growth to become the best version of herself. She thrives when she's encouraging, empowering, supporting and uplifting others. She loves being a coach for others as she believes every individual that finds their inner purpose and allows their truest self to shine through can do massive, life changing things. Nicole knows the importance of self-care and she does that best by grounding herself in nature. She recharges herself by doing nothing, but breathing in the fresh air with the people she loves most. She loves caring and pampering others which led her to her esthetics career. She loves to let her creative energies flow, by writing, do-it-yourself projects, painting and crafting. Nicole loves to push herself out of her comfort zone to try new things. Nicole has this fire and determination to share her story so that she can spread hope and the importance of never giving up to anyone who is going through anything along their journey through life.

ACKNOWLEDGEMENTS

I would like to acknowledge my husband, Andrew. My rock, soul mate, best friend and biggest supporter. You're the best husband and dad and I am so grateful for you; your courage, strength, wisdom and this beautiful life we created together and our ability to never quit. Thank you for always believing in me and my abilities even when I didn't believe in myself. My son, Wyatt, I am forever grateful that you chose us to be your parents. You are a light in this world. You're so handsome, smart, kind, brave, strong, empathetic; you have the biggest heart and you made our world complete. Tiffany, my sister and best friend, you have been one of the biggest supports for me during this entire journey and I am so grateful for you. Thank you for your strength and courage to be there the moment my son took his first breath. To my mom (Cathy), mother-in-law (Dawne), dad (Tony), father-in-law (Steve) your unconditional love and strength has been a guiding light, you have lifted me up during some of my most difficult times and I love and appreciate you all. To everyone else who has been on this journey with me, thank you.

With gratitude,
Nicole Recker

Feel free to connect with Nicole Recker!

Instagram
@nicolereckersjourney
@thegreaterplanbook

Facebook
@NicoleCRecker

Websites:
www.nicolerecker.com
www.nicoledavis2.arbonne.com

If you enjoyed this book, I'd be honoured if you'd spend a few minutes writing a review on Amazon.

Manufactured by Amazon.ca
Bolton, ON

36246024R00083